Lights in the Mountains

Lights in the Mountains

Stories, Essays and Poems by Writers Living in and Inspired by the Southern Appalachian Mountains

Edited by Nancy Simpson and Shirley Uphouse

with an introduction by North Carolina Poet Laureate, Fred Chappell

Stories chosen by Ruth Moose
Essays chosen by Steven Harvey
Poems chosen by Kathryn Stripling Byer

Winding Path Publishing

First edition

This literary collection contains the work of fifty-three authors including an introduction by Fred Chappell.

ISBN 0-9740376-0-5

Cover photo by Mary Ricketson

Winding Path Publishing
North Carolina Writers' Network West
472 Old Cherry Mountain Trail
Hayesville, NC 28904
www.ncwriters.org

Published in the United States of America.

Dedication

Doris Buchanan Smith

June 1, 1934–August 8, 2002

This anthology, *Lights in the Mountains,* is dedicated to the memory of Doris Buchanan Smith, author of seventeen novels for adolescents. Her classic, *A Taste of Blackberries (Thomas Y. Crowell Co., New York 1973)* broke literary ground by being the first childrens' book in which a child as a main character dies. *A Taste of Blackberries,* published in ten languages, received the Children's Book Award, The Child Study Award and was named an American Language Association Notable Book.

Doris Buchanan Smith spent the last twenty-seven years of her life writing on Cherry Mountain near Hayesville, North Carolina. She was a member of the North Carolina Writers' Network and a friend and mentor to mountain writers.

Acknowledgements:

This anthology was published with the full sponsorship of the North Carolina Writers' Network Board of Directors which acts as fiscal agent for this project. We thank them all.

Members of the North Carolina Writers' Network West conceived this anthology and it was accomplished through their efforts and input. Our sincere thanks to the Anthology Committee, to Paul Donovan, Committee Chairman and to many from the general membership for their help to bring this book to print.

Our deep gratitude goes to North Carolina Poet Laureate Fred Chappell for his generous introductory comments.

We appreciate Steven Harvey who chose the essays, Kathryn Stripling Byer who chose the poems and Ruth Moose who chose the short stories. We thank them for letting us include a sample of their excellent works.

Acknowledgement for previously copyrighted and/or previously published material: *Southern Humanities Review* (Spring 1982) for "Under the Earth" by Janice Townley Moore; University of South Carolina Press for "The Garden Wall" from *A Geometry of Lilies: Life and Death in An American Family* by Steven Harvey; *Appalachian Heritage* for "Antiques" by Estelle Darrow Rice; *Freeing Jonah III* for "Applebutter Time" by Joyce Foster; *Jonah* IV for "Picture Window" by Ralph B. Montee; *August House* for "Wreath Ribbon Quilt" by Ruth Moose from the short story collection by the same title; *Blue Ridge Guide 1994* and *Stoneflower Literary Journal 1998* for "I'll Be Home for Christmas" by Jerry R. Houser; *Smoky Mountain News* for "Musings on Love, Rain, a Few Poems and Adolescents" by Dawn Gilchrist-Young; *Synergy* for "An Emerald Cloak, Trimmed in White" by John Webb; *Independence Boulevard* for "Funerals Are for the Living" by Mary E. Lynn Drew; L.S.U. Press for "Ivory Combs" from *Wildwood Flower* by Kathryn Stripling Byer; *Southern Humanities Review* for "Detours" by Carol Crawford.

Contents:

Introduction

by Fred Chappell

Once upon a time an anthology like the one you now hold in your hands would be almost entirely predictable in content. The poems would be mostly set in hymn meter and concern themselves with nature in her gentler aspects, with religions and family devotion. Now and then a timid but flowery love poem might rear a blushing countenance. The prose would consist of character portraits--usually of revered elder figures, grandparents and mothers, a father or two of either the hardworking or hard-drinking persuasion. Accounts of spiritual conversion would appear and animal stories, probably about hunting or fishing, many dogs and a few cats.

Those are steady and durable themes and they are plentiful in *Lights in the Mountains* and the authors have given them worthy treatments. But here you will also find stories of life in other places, in military service abroad or in more familiar American scenes distant from the mountains of western North Carolina. Traditional themes receive untraditional presentations; the love poems speak more frankly than in former decades and the love stories often deal with separation. The influence of the Nashville jukebox can be heard in some of the wryer lines. And that good old standby, the glory of Appalachian nature, is seen as a more fragile subject than it once was, endangered by many forces, not all of them from "outside."

But verities remain verities and our writers stand to the truth of what they have witnessed, thought and felt. Debora Kinsland Foerst's poem, "Lights in the Smokies", tells of those mysterious nocturnal lights in the mountains that only special people can see and identifies them as protectors of Appalachian culture and the Appalachian landscape. The title of this book, *Lights in the Mountains*, refers to these fugitive gleams but also implies that the writers represented here are lights that illuminate and, by flashing warnings, try to protect.

And if it is true that only special people may notice these lights or add to their luminance, that is no cause for grave concern. It has always been left to a small number of individuals to stand watch, to make art from closely observed materials, to celebrate whatever cries out its need to be celebrated, joyfully or tragically. When we read this book we add ourselves to that limited company, a proud one to be in.

–And then, of course, there is also a great deal of fun in these pages!

Telling

by Linda Taylor Kane

It comes to me sometimes,
what happened,

but when summer haze
wraps around these mountains
making them reflections
of the ones behind them, you can't tell
if they're fibbing about themselves,
or if they're really there.
They drape like drowsy shadows,
as though you could see right through them
if you just stared hard enough.

That's when I start to question:
Did it happen that way?

But the next morning when I wake up,
the day will be clear and cool.
Each one of these hills will be
right where it has always been,
its crisp blues and greens reaching up,
claiming its own named place.

Just so you know, when I'm telling you,
it's all in how the light plays.

1

Under the Earth

by Janice Townley Moore

Where the road slices
through Needle Gorge
animals of stone
root out of the cliff.

Their snouts, heads, shoulders
bulge from red clay
as if to catch the scent of
ancient water.

Eons piled upon eons
this is the only place
where the mountain lion
will lie with the lamb.

Stacked together,
the buffalo, wild boar,
oxen, the goat
with its grassy beard—

Did they all stop
before they reached
the saving water of the river,
caught in their final breath?

Those Smoky Bears

by Margaret Lynn Brown

Will Thomas is late again, and you know how men are: you give 'em twenty minutes this time, then it's thirty minutes next time, and soon you're sitting all night by the phone with a diet soda thinking how lousy it tastes, and now that he's gone, who cares about diets anyway?

And so I take off, pretty as you please, and before you can say "hey" I'm driving north on I-26 bound for the state of Tennessee. Ever since Roy left, I have worn a groove between my house and my sister's, April Jean's, in Knoxville. It's not so much visiting my sister as the drive: a ribbon of asphalt that climbs into the heavens and wraps itself around the free world as we know it. If I could just think of someplace else to go, I wouldn't end up stuck there in the living room of that split-level with my brother-in-law, three kids, and stain-free plush pile carpeting; how anyone can vacuum all those damn stairs I have no idea.

Anyway, Will Thomas is late again, this time thirty minutes, and it's important not to give men the idea you'll wait for them, so my firm rule is to drive away, then return and pretend that you only just now remembered he was expected. "Are you always this punctual?" I'll say, surprised. "If you don't mind waiting, I just need a moment to freshen up." *Hah! Chew on that for a while.* I floor the Toyota and pass a couple of people from Michigan or Minnesota or someplace like that.

How I do love these hills, these green North Carolina hills, the way the four-lane rolls straight toward the gaps. "Jesus is Lord Over North Carolina," says the bumper sticker in front of me. I honk and wave at an elderly couple in a pick-up truck. This Toyota has a little spirit yet. Take *that* Mr. Highway Patrol!

You know what I'm going to do? I'm going to skip April Jean's house and turn into the Smoky Mountains. I'm going to walk down the street in Gatlinburg and buy me a little black bear on a stick. I do love those bears. Once when I was seven, before Daddy died, Mama and Daddy took us to Gatlinburg, and Lord, Lord, how I loved those bears. The real ones I mean. April Jean and I bought Ritz crackers to feed the bears, because we found they prefer Ritz crackers to soda crackers or even Oreo cookies. The bears came right up to the station wagon, and we screamed as their claws scratched at the windows. Daddy got out to provide a diversion, and Mama began banging on the roof of the car with her brown alligator-look bag. Daddy yelled for Mama to stay in the car, then Mama's handbag burst and spilled the entire contents onto 441. I saved the day by throwing the box of Ritz crackers up the hill, but no one remembers that Nadine Ann is the hero of this story. It has been told several ways by Mama and April Jean. Neither of them ever end it with me saving us all. Since Daddy died, there is just no one to support my version of things.

Take for example the second time April Jean and I went to the Smoky Mountains after her high school graduation. We were sailing along like I am now, probably arguing about who saved us from the bears, when I suddenly realized that I passed a highway patrolman. Before I could slow down, we were being chased with lights and a siren like common criminals.

"What seems to be the trouble, sir," I asked the officer, a tall man who walked as if his pants were too tight.

"Ma'am, you were edging 80 in a 65 mph zone," he answered. Now these are the facts of the story that April Jean and I agree on. In her version, though, she puts on a voice that is supposed to be mine and squeals like Scarlet O'Hara: "Is that right? I just don't know how that could *be*."

"Well, er...yes Ma'am...er Miss."

"I mean, my sister and I...April Jean...this is my sister here, April Jean, who has recently become a graduate of high school."

"Nice to meet you," the officer said, crouching to tip his Smoky the Bear hat.

"She's the sweetest girl, and single too I might add," I supposedly said. "April Jean and I were just discussing how the speed limit surely needs to be lowered what with all these reports coming out about automobiles being unsafe at any speed. Don't you agree?"

"Well, I guess I haven't given it much thought."

"Of course, it might make your job a whole lot more difficult, what with the way people like to speed."

"I try to enforce the law."

"I understand that, I certainly do. I genuinely apologize, sir, if I have violated statues."

"Uh...perhaps there's something wrong with your speedometer? Have you had it checked lately?"

"You know I don't know. We did have the spark plugs changed before we left," I said, "according to my sister." Now when April

Jean tells this story, she will add all manner of eye fluttering and further ridiculous motions with her hands, but I know that I did not try to manipulate that officer in any way.

I got off with a warning. To top it off, the officer was so mixed up that he wrote "Ann" as my first name and "Nadine" as my last, forgetting the surname altogether. At that moment, I made one of two mistakes in my life: I handed the receipt to April Jean, who has saved it in her billfold ever since. She brings it out as verification whenever this story is mentioned. When she told Roy he laughed until he was sick to his stomach. After I divorced Roy and started dating Will Thomas, she told him too. He jiggled that old, big belly and tried to wink at me.

The second mistake of my life was, of course, marrying Roy. My foot hits the gas as I think of this worthless example of mankind to whom I offered up the best years of my life. No, not exactly. The best years of my life were spent sitting next to Daddy on the front porch, and now that I think of it, they may have ended with the spark plug story, because shortly thereafter Roy asked me to the drive-in. Six months later we were married and shortly after started bickering. Roy stayed ten years, then he ran off with the Italian woman who owns the Used A Bit shop. Just like a man to run off when the going gets tough.

I cut on the radio. "When you find another friend who lights your candle up again, burn one down for me," sings Clint Black. I switch stations. "Got no one to call my own no more," Dolly wails. I light a cigarette. What a whiner. Dolly has enough money to buy the county she was born in, and we're supposed to feel sorry for her.

"It's just a song," Roy would say, whenever I expressed my irritation with music.

"It's the principle, Roy. We're paying good money to hear this woman cry about old Jolene, some whore whose hustling Dolly's man while she's off traveling the country making television specials. Why doesn't she just stay home and attend to business. I don't feel sorry for her."

"Woman, you bleed my brains dry," Roy would say.

"Woman, you bleed my brains dry," were, in fact, the last words Roy spoke on the morning of July 9th when he strode off the porch, never to be heard from again, except through friends who reported on his whereabouts. Eleven years of your life you spend confessing your sins to someone, and he leaves you to set up company with a Used A Bit woman.

On my first date with Will Thomas, I retold this entire story. He nodded, then recalled how after his wife died, he missed the way she accidentally busted the egg yolks when she cooked for him. What kind of a comment was that? Men are truly the mental midgets of the human race. I offer the most heart-breaking moment of my life, and all he can think about is egg yolk.

"You're just lucky he asked you out again, girl," Mama said on the phone the next day. "I told you not to talk about Roy on the first date. Men hate to think they're getting used goods."

"Recycled, Mama."

"At this rate you're going to be an antique."

"They go for high prices."

Mama favored Will Thomas from the beginning. She called it *mother's intuition*, and because she got to April Jean first, both of them were on his side. This bothers me, because this same conspiracy blames me for letting Roy run off with a junk woman. When I told Mama and April Jean about that day Roy left, I let it slip that I thought Roy was just on his way to Hardee's, which proved what they suspected all along: I did not ordinarily get up and fix Roy breakfast. Then Roy spread it to the rest of humanity that I slept in curlers, which is untrue, but they believed it.

"There is simply no excuse for curlers," April Jean said for no particular reason one night when we were watching TV, "in this day and decade when electric rollers and curling irons are so commonly available. Most women would pay for a perm before they would let their husbands see them in curlers."

"Even the most difficult man can be trained to eat cereal for breakfast if you're short on time," Mama said for no particular reason one evening when we were washing soup greens.

Just thinking about her comment makes me swerve around a semi-trailer, which honks, so I soar past the entire convoy. "Every time you drive this car you put an American out of work," Roy told me whenever he rode in the Toyota. But Lord I love this car. A woman and her Toyota take Tennessee! I drop the cigarette butt in the ash tray and sing along with Patty Loveless: "Chains, chains, shackles and chains, some day I'm gonna break these..." Hello, Smoky Mountains, goodbye, Will Thomas!

What frustrates me about this man can be understood by our trip to Winn-Dixie yesterday. We pulled up in the Toyota: Will Thomas, me, and Mama, who's wearing a pink plaid house dress with matching shoes and purse. I got a shopping cart, then realized that Will Thomas and Mama were nowhere to be seen. I squinted my eyes and saw Mama still in the Toyota, down on her hands and knees, cleaning out my floorboards, with her pink plaid behind sticking out the door.

Will Thomas hung there by the car, like some kind of refugee.

"What, are, you, doing, Mama?" I did not have a measure of patience left.

"What have you been transporting, girl?" Mama held up little pieces of grass and twigs.

"Mama, will you kindly get up and stop making a spectacle of me in the Winn-Dixie parking lot?"

"What is poor Will Thomas to think, Nadine?" We both turned and looked at him. It was a long minute. Slowly, Will Thomas began to make an escape, sidling up to the sidewalk, darting around half-price lawn furniture toward the entrance of the supermarket. "Now, look what you've done," Mama said.

I can get along without a damn refugee. I can get along, thank you very much, without a man who prefers to spend his evenings eating spaghetti on the other side of town. And if Mama and April Jean would rather believe these men than their own flesh and blood, nothing can be done about it. One hour from now I will be in a cabin outside Gatlinburg, sipping a raspberry wine cooler and feeding the bears Ritz crackers in the sunset.

"Damn," I say, and it is not a pretty sound. Damn! Damn! Damn! I have somehow just passed a highway patrolman. I have been thinking too much to know how fast I'm traveling. "Never drive when you're angry," the South's Number One Psychic once told me. And then something happens that never happens to me; my throat is choked shut with a lump the size of your fist.

I dig through my handbag for my driver's license. "Do not cry, girl, whatever you do, do not cry," I repeat to myself as I fling aside nail files and empty Virginia Slim packages. I slip my card through a crack in the window, repeating to myself, "do not cry, do not cry, do not cry."

The patrolman can't be over twenty-one.

"Good evening, Ma'am, where are you headed?"

"My sister's--Knoxville."

"I know how it is, Ma'am, you get in a hurry on a Friday--weekend. But Ma'am, you were driving 14 mph over the speed limit."

"I'm sorry," I say, but it doesn't get around the lump.

"Excuse me, Ma'am?"

"Iggsmmph," I blubber.

"Now, Ma'am, don't you worry, we all make mistakes. I just have to run your tag through our computers to make sure you don't have any outstanding warrants. It's my job."

"Damn! Damn! Damn!" I bang my forehead against the steering wheel, and the tears run down the sides of my thighs. I hate you, Will Thomas.

"Everything looks fine," the young man returns. "I'll let you off with a warning this time. I need you to sign here....I hope that the rest of your evening is better than this." He waits for me to drive off the shoulder first. I wipe my face with my sleeve and proceed cautiously off the gravel. At the next exit, I pull into the Cracker Barrel, wash my face and re-apply make-up. At the check-out, I pass a display of homemade fudge, which is Will Thomas' favorite, which he does not need, a man with a belly that size.

After spending my last dollar on fudge I march back to the Toyota. I face the Smoky Mountains. Then I turn, and roar back down the four-lane, praying...that man and his belly are still on my front porch.

Full Circle

by Pat Workman

My thoughts rumble when thunder
vaults the Nantahala mountains.
My nostrils fill with smell of sweat
soaked leather. Blowing rain
becomes a horse's mane slapping
me back to range those salty hills
with the Mormon Sons of Daniel.

I must have been a Danite
with ten wives to glean my hay,
ten guns to fire in the name of God,
ten horses to guard my boundaries,
and ten hundred heirs
to insure my grip upon the land.

In this Appalachian lifetime,
I am a lone wife
living with a man who needs ten.
Now for need of space, I fire words,
teach my sons that we can never
own a single grain of sand.

The Garden Wall

by Steven Harvey

Last year it was mulch. I lugged the woods' dead leavings in a wheelbarrow, hugged the loamy mix of soil and bark and rot against my chest, breathing the woodsy musk, spread each load over the shovel-chopped red clay of out gardens and spent the spring consumed by thoughts of mortality. This year it is stone. I'm building a garden wall. My mortarless monument makes its way across the front of our house beneath a bay window and hems in the mulch of last year's garden. Stone by stone it has grown under my hands, changing character as I go: a crude cluster of hardened sinners expanding slowly into a dignified pew of solid citizens.

It changes, too, according to the weather. On clear days the wall sheds its dutiful look, becoming younger and oddly softer in sunlight, glistening like the scrubbed faces of naughty choirboys glancing this way and that. On rainy days it has a monkish air, the jumbled stones a solemn row of cowled heads, bowed or hung or jauntily erect as dignity demands and piety allows. Who knows what thoughts consume them? I'm only half through making the low structure, and already it has redefined our house, rounding off sharp corners so that the place looks less new, and a little more world-weary. Often after spending a long day working there I find myself wasting the evening sitting on the stones, thoughts of mortality arriving again, but in new robes now as darkness seeps into the sloping lawn like the slow advance of mourners and the hum of the woods takes on the heaviness of chapel bells.

There is nothing to building a wall–nothing, that is, except muscle and patience. To get started, I slip on gloves, grab the handle of the plastic cart, and head for the hillside. Sometimes I leave the gloves behind. I like the cart's bump and clank as I walk down the graveled drive, my clatter dissipating into woods and sky as if this were play, though I know full well that the return trip will be all creaks and groans and funereal rumblings.

Along the way I pass a gravesite on a property near ours. River stones, pocked and mossy, sit upright there at the head and foot of graves more than a hundred years old, the whole site of five or six plots marked by orange plastic flags. Surveyors discovered the neglected graves when staking for a house and were forbidden by local laws to proceed with building, the stones of the dead laying claim to the land of the living.

I rarely go past the spot without stopping, paying my respects by standing among the squared-off slabs of river rock. Nothing can be read on the weathered markers, nothing except the simple fact that whatever and whoever happened here ended *here*. Who were they? Poor white immigrants who turned up these boulders when ploughing fields? Runaway slaves who left little trace of their existence except rocks and bones? *Bones*, I think, rattling past. The stones that we carry in us all our lives, stones that rise out of us when we die.

Stones do, in fact, rise. Water collects beneath them and freezes, the ice lifting a new crop to the surface each year. In the mountains the rocks emerge only to be washed downhill by spring rains. They collect about the trunks of trees as if stones, like pups around a bitch, need to huddle about something alive for nourishment. There they remain for the lifetime of the tree–draped in the mulch of a hundred seasons–until the trunk cracks and tumbles and rots, so that the rocks can begin, again, the millennial journey to the creek.

When I get to the site, I leave my cart behind in the road and traipse uphill looking for rocky hiding places. Cold pearls for a warm neck, I think, coming upon stones piled about a beech. One by one I pry them from their ancient settings. I like flat stones, so I only take the ones that lift easily out of the dirt–a simple chore. Inevitably I expose scurrying underlife–slugs, dung beetles, worms, and snakes all snuggling into mud burrows or wriggling into holes. My dream life, I know, has become richer since I started digging, my dark hours haunted by slimy burrowers and centipeded creatures in sectional carapaces. Subterranean spirits at work in the soil are at work in me too.

A stone wall does not require work. It *means* work, as John Jerome puts it in his book *Stone Work*. Agony, I think, is a better word–Greek for struggle. English for pain. In stonework, flesh finds rock, vulnerability meets durability and the result is a scrape and a scar. Like a leaf blown against a chain fence in the rain or a body dragged under a bumper, an inevitable yielding occurs when I brace my legs and lift a stone out of the cart. Under the weight I feel a give in my body opening a passageway to mysteries. Lifting the rock to my shoulder, I think of the hand raised in the cave at Lascaux, dying the calcified interior with life's colors, a hand that later raised stones against the woolly mammoth trapped in a rocky cul-de-sac.

Cherokees who lived here more than a hundred and fifty years ago considered the earth sacred. When they moved a stone, they apologized to the ground. I lift the stones out of their dirt beds with little more than a groan on my lips. Like the rootless teeth of babies, they rise out of the gums of earth where they have lain for an eternity, gray and pocked on one side with lichen, those fingerprint whorls that rocks acquire in the woods, and on the underside brown and red with clay. These I rub with my gloves, raise high in the air, and throw downhill. They rumble and skid to a stop against tree or mound or, running out of steam, pause upright, then tilt into the weeds. In a moment the excitement is over and they are still again, ready, if necessary, to wait out another eternity.

The Cherokees knew about the deadly durability of stone: arrowheads sown into the nearby corn and sorghum fields have *forever* scalloped into each flint shard. Before the Cherokees, the mound builders shaped the earth itself, creating enormous, enduring earthen graves on the landscape. At a spot on the Arkaqua trail, not far from where I live, is a hillside littered with huge, soapstone rocks, gray-black boulders that rise like the backs of dolphins out of the leaf-littered slope. We call the place Track Rock because some of the stones bear the marks of ancient, nameless Indian tribes, marks which by legend are the tracks of fleeing animals. Souvenir hunters have chiseled away chunks of Track Rock and acid rain has pocked the stone surface, but some tracks remain as ghostly, smooth-edged versions of the originals.

"The carvings are of many and various patterns," James Mooney notes in *Myths of the Cherokee*, "some of them resembling human or animal footprints, while others are squares, crosses, circles, 'bird tracks' . . . disposed without any apparent order." When I run my fingers over the indentations, the shapes large and deep enough to hold a hand, I think of the Indian name for the spot, Branded Place, and feel the age-old ambition of humans to lay claim to nature by shaping its stones, the sympathetic magic which insists that the earth and its beasts accept the human imprint, the brand, before the kill.

According to myth, animals left many of these markings on the stones during the great southern migration. Ayasta, the only woman at the beginning of this century privileged to speak in council among the East Cherokees, claimed that the animals at one time suffered famine in the mountains. According to the tale, Grubworm and Woodchuck held council and sent Pigeon in search of food. She flew south and found abundant grain fields, so the animals migrated into the low country–an army of beasts. Mythic hunters had no choice but to follow, accounting for the footprints and handprints in stone. I imagine the circle of Indian faces, streaked with resins, and see skin lit by sputtering fires. I imagine the spears tipped with stone.

Scholarship on Track Rock suggests a more lowly origin; Mooney quoted "sensible Indians" who said that bored hunters chipped out the animal tracks *for their own amusement.* Maybe. One of the endearing qualities of the Cherokees is their humor, their willingness to poke fun at their own myths, and maybe the earlier tribe shared this playful spirit. Nevertheless, I am suspicious of the word *sensible,* here, suggesting as it does that the common sense of outsiders can penetrate the uncommon mysteries of another culture. Whether it is true or not, though–whether this is an example of magic beyond our comprehension or America's original graffiti–the ambition to lay claim to forever is the same. Here warm hand met cold stone; the result was a scar.

Stonework can scar more than hands and stone, of course, sometimes taking a toll on machines as well. Several days into the wall project my cart broke down. I had piles in the usual load of stones and, positioned like a donkey at the front, yanked as hard as I could. Nothing budged. When I turned back to check out the problem, I found the cart beached in the dirt, axle to the ground and wheels splayed like flippers on both sides. After I emptied the load and turned over the whole mess, the source of the problem was clear: too many heavy loads had caused the metal bolts to wobble, leaving wide gaps in the plastic, and the chassis had pulled loose from the wheelbase. The cart lies now on my basement workbench, resting in pieces.

I began hauling stones in our car, loading the trunk with rock and driving the short distance from hill to wall, but this led to other casualties. Under the weight of a load of stones, the tires dug trenches in our lawn, and rocks tore at the rubber seals of the trunk, ripping one strip out like an umbilical cord and scratching and denting the metal rim. One rock slipped from my hands, flopped down the hill, bounded up a gully, turned on its axis and tumbled–punch drunk–against the bumper of the car.

Yet somehow these rocks, disciplined and chastened into a wall, seem worth the agony, especially at the end of the day when breezes let the sweat dry cool on my neck and five-year-old Alice brings me a beer from the kitchen before dancing off to play with the dog. My stones and I seem like war buddies then–or even better, like illicit lovers, having hugged and grappled with each other only to find that the affair has changed us in different ways, one scrubbed and the other sullied by the experience.

Stone walls have a long shelf life, so I expect these old friends to outlast me, which is an odd comfort. I walk past an old home site nearby, the house long gone, replaced by a new trailer. A hundred feet away, a stone wall—older than the trailer, house, or inhabitants—encircles a stump of morning glories and remains intact. I'll go like the stump, I say to myself, walking on. I'll crack at the back and rot from within, leaving Alice to brighten the walls of our making.

Not long ago Dad called, his raspy voice gravelly and somber. His dog, a beloved pet, had died, and he suggested that my family delay a planned visit. My dad is the kind of no-nonsense businessman who uses the word *thing* for whatever is inexplicable. "This thing has really gotten to your mother," he said. "She needs a break."

The dog, a bichon frise that had lived with them for five years and accompanied them on a difficult move from Florida to Kentucky, had been a white froth of energy in their lives when my father's diabetes grew serious and his heartbeat unsteady. All gestures for Dad had become studied and slow, and each one no doubt required just as much effort and concentration from my stepmother, who registered his every move in her mind and heart. Mom cried a lot over the phone. "It's just one of those things," my dad would say.

Now their dog, the one bit of fluff in their lives, had contracted cancer. They kept it alive until the wound was an open sore, a knot of pain, and no anodyne helped. Eventually Mom took the dog to the vet and had it put to sleep. When the vet injected the lethal dose, my mother, holding the dog on the table, screamed and ran from the room, frightening everyone, including herself.

When I got her on the phone her voice sounded subdued, weary, the words sliding away from the ledge of sound like scree shaken loose from a hillside. "Your Dad's taking this real hard," she said. "That dog got him through all those attacks."

Last year my dad had a defibrillator inserted surgically into his chest, a rock-hard device sewn under the skin that clicks in and takes over when his heart stops. The first time it worked he was elated and called in a celebratory mood to tell us the good news—"I guess I would have been a goner without it," he said in a flinty voice—but since then the device has weighed him down. Going off often and regularly, it no longer reassures but serves instead as a reminder of vulnerability.

"We'll get through this thing," Dad says now, if I ask.

"He'll miss his little friend," my mother says, her voice brittle and cracked, and I know suddenly the adamantine silences at the far ledge of love.

Sometimes Alice helps me by lugging stones. Setting her trembling lips and squinting her eyes, she lifts a small rock out of the cart, tottering under her load for a step of two before letting it plop, at last, to the ground. "There!" she says. The rest of the time she leans against the wall or stretches out on a large brown capstone, her body all soft flesh, glowing, evanescent in the sun. She chatters away about butterflies while I pass before her–blue-faced and ladened and leaden. Someday, perhaps, she will build *her* wall while *I* watch.

A stone wall is never just stone: an eye envisions it, a hand shapes it, and a mind holds the boulders in place. Humanity insinuates itself into the ten-ton, gap-toothed smile that crosses an empty field, a monument to flesh and blood as well as bone. Like a poem, a stone wall holds fragility in place, each word mossy on the surface but hard at the core, the whole a solid but serpentine creation of mind and heart. The word *poem* comes, in fact, from an ancient root meaning, "one stone piled on another." Plowshares turned up stones and these made their way to the poems that held down the corners of our fields long ago.

So at the end of each day I stand back, exhausted, and admire the poetry of my handiwork. Like books crowded along shelves, the neat rows of chunky and lean volumes yanked one way and another by gaps and crowding, this library of the inarticulate hours bears the imprint of its maker and says all I know about eternity.

It has been my habit each night after finishing a section to pop a beer and sit among my rocky brethren, the cowled fraternity. From my cool seat I look out on the living figures in the evening lawn–grass, flower, cocker, girl. Groundhog, bear, squirrel–and who knows what else–watch silently from the margin. A line of darkness crosses the field, and the tapestry darkens at the edges as woods and nighttime eat into the fabric of the day. My wall is the last to go, the shadows edging up my pant leg before blanketing the stones in gray.

I'm big on commemorations–my meager attempts to hang onto the now–so I've already developed plans for celebrating the wall when it's done. On that evening when I wedge the last stone in place, I will without fanfare conduct my ceremony and pour what's left of the beer over the rocky-hided spirit of my creation. Banishing all thoughts of mortality for the moment, I'll watch soft follow hard, as the liquid trickles down stoney sides. Absorbing nothing and exposing all, the stones hauled by my hands will remain unmoved–my offering of cool, wet pleasures bleeding at length into the black, thirsty mulch below.

Lights in the Smokies

by Debora Kinsland Foerst

Granny Myrt says the lights protect,
but only special people can see the lights
because the lights are really flames from fires
set in our mountains by medicine men.

But only special people can see the lights
shimmering at Straight Fork, Bigwitch, the Kituwah mound
set in our mountains by medicine men.
Something had to be done after the Removal.

Shimmering at Straight Fork, Bigwitch, the Kituwah mound.
People are still greedy.
Something had to be done after the Removal
to keep and protect what little we had left.

People are still greedy.
Strong Medicine had to be used
to keep and protect what little we had left.
They doctored our mountains.

Strong medicine had to be used
because the lights are really flames from fires.
They doctored our mountains.
Granny Myrt says the lights protect.

Mamaw's Porch

by Glenda Barrett

To a stranger there would be nothing special about the porch that ran across the front of my grandmother's house. It was not one of those smooth, polished porches with large columns you might see in a magazine. Actually, it was constructed with concrete that in later years cracked leaving an ugly scar running through the middle of it. Many times I've heard my grandmother say, "That porch really needs fixing." The front door to the white, shingled house was positioned in the center of the porch, and on either side of the door sat two large rocking chairs each one large enough for two people to sit in comfortably.

Over the years the porch was a busy place. One of the main attractions to the porch was my grandmother's flowers. Not only had she planted flowers in the yard near the porch, but she also had potted plants around the inside of the porch. Since I lived within walking distance to her house, I visited her often. She was always glad to see me.

"Let me show you my flowers," she said every time. I'd follow her out on the porch and watch as she bent down and touched the leaves as if they were small children. I can hear her now, "Glenda, come look at my pink double begonia!" Being young and energetic, there were days I wasn't too interested in her flowers, but to please her, I looked anyway.

During gardening time she would take her bucket of green beans to the porch, scoop some up in her apron and begin to string them for dinner. She worked in a slow, easy manner as if it was a pleasure. Never in my life did I see her do a chore any other way. I'd reach over in her lap, pick up a few beans to help. She listened while I talked, and soon I'd ask, "Mamaw, do you know any good stories?"

From her porch I've heard her predict the weather many times over the years.

"I believe we'll have a storm before the day's over," she'd say. "See those mare's tails in the sky." She referred to the white wisps of clouds in the sky that resembled a mare's tail. Often, in the evenings, as the sun began to go down, she watched the pink color on the horizon over the Blue Ridge Mountains and cited, "Red clouds in the morning, a shepherd's warning, red clouds at night, a shepherd's delight."

In the morning, as the fog lifted, I could see the tips of the mountains peeping through, and the damp pastures glistened as the sun slipped over the mountain ridges. If I looked close enough, I could see the tower of Bald Mountain from her porch.

It was evenings that I loved best, especially those in the spring of the year. Frogs croaked in the nearby stream signaling the end of winter. As summer approached, I loved to watch the lightning bugs flicker over the yard in the dark. Sometimes, I caught a few and put them in a pint jar. Later, I felt sorry for them and let them go.

Mamaw was a real expert on telling ghost stories, and if she told one at night it was a scary thing to walk home. In order to get there, I had to pass an old chicken house on one side of the road and a leaning, gray barn on the other side. With my vivid imagination, I pictured all sorts of things among the dark shadows. I heard my sister say once that she did not walk but ran all the way home after hearing Mamaw tell one of her ghost stories.

In the summer, the porch caused a bit of anxiety especially before the family reunion. Mamaw was an excellent housekeeper, and about a week before the reunion she said, "Glenda, we've got to get this house cleaned up before all the relatives come to visit. It is a scandal! And those porches will have to be scrubbed." She referred to the back porch as well, the one where she fed her stray cats and dogs.

Over the years, I watched her nurse many stray and sick animals back to health. I remember one kitten she named, "Lucy," and she talked about it in such a loving manner, a stranger would have thought it was a person.

On the back porch, she kept her crooked, cane fishing pole and bait cans. In the summer, she'd look up at the sky and say,

"Glenda, I believe today might be a good fishing day. Don't you?" We'd get our poles and walk the short distance across the highway down through the pasture to the nearby creek. Each time I came back with a dose of poison ivy, while Mamaw always had a nice string of bream. After our trip she'd sit down in her rickety chair on the back porch while we talked about our trip and divided the fish.

Mamaw cared for herself and her house until she was close to ninety years old. She then realized she could no longer do it anymore and admitted herself to the nursing home. However, she instructed my aunt to keep the electricity on in case she wanted to come back home. In a few months she did want to come home for a visit. My cousin brought her home, and she looked through the house as if she had never seen it before. Later, I remember her telling me that she had counted eleven family members that came to visit that day. She sat in her favorite chair and hummed some old hymns while my sister played the piano. Mamaw savored every minute of it. At the end of the day, before she had to go back to the nursing home, she walked out on the porch, looked around at what was left of her flowers and the yard, turned to her family and said, "My time is up, it's time to go."

Time has passed now and so has Mamaw. I live about five miles from her old home place. Last summer her house and properties were sold, and for a time, as I passed her home, I saw a few of her flowers still growing in the yard. I still long to sit one more time on Mamaw's front porch and rest beside her. Just one more time I wish I could say "Mamaw, do you know any good stories?"

Garden

by Mary Peavey Ricketson

Hot sun beats upon beads
of sweat rolling down my head.
Shards of dirt fall
from my feet and fingers.
From toil and pleasure
deep in blackest earth
come roots of finest food.
From sweat and dirt
comes cleansing
of my heart and soul,
in ceremony
that marries me to life itself.

Like A Band of Miniature Angels

by Shirley Uphouse

When my sister, Pat, was seven and I was nine we were introduced to some old time religion we shall never forget. Until then we hadn't attended church often. We lived a few miles from town, and our old automobile was rarely operational. On the heels of the Great Depression, money for repairs was tight, and Father spent more time under the car than in it.

Still, Mother felt Pat and I should attend Sunday school, so when a friend told her about his church that picked up folks in their bus on Sunday mornings, Mother made plans for us to attend. The following Sunday we waited by the mailbox wearing our best dresses and clutching a dime each for the collection plate. This was our first bus ride, and we were titillated with our new adventure. The moment we climbed into the old battered bus we were enveloped in *Hallelujahs!, Amens*! and *Praise the Lords!* As the bus rounded the corner by the apple orchard, we looked back to see Mother still waving.

The little church sat back in the hills, down a narrow dirt road. It was a small wooden building, clean but spartan. There were no stained glass windows, no steeple, no padded pew seats. Electricity hadn't found its way to this corner of the county, and smoky kerosene lamps hung from the ceiling. Without inside plumbing, we used the little house out back. But all this humble house of worship lacked in amenities was surpassed with enthusiasm and a love of mankind among its faithful congregation.

Sunday school was fun: stories, coloring books, cookies. After class, and eager to join the other adults, our teacher took us into the church to attend the regular service. It was not yet noon, but the dog days of August were upon us, and the sanctuary was stifling. Hand-held paper fans advertising Bramley's Funeral Home fluttered throughout the church like a band of miniature angels. While we'd been in class, the adults had gotten a good start on praising the Lord and damning the devil.

The preacher, tall and lean, his face flushed and dripping perspiration, implored us sinners to save ourselves and join him up front to receive the Lord. A few repentant souls went forward. Pat and I giggled when a man fell down at the preacher's feet, arms and legs flailing about, uttering a jumble of strange words. Looking about,

21

we saw no one else was amused. Soon a very large woman went forward, stepped onto the platform and collapsed against the podium, eyes raised to the heavens, tears rolling down her tormented face. This was nothing like the sedate services at the First Presbyterian church in town. We were wide-eyed and consumed by the show.

After the preacher had lifted each saved soul, blessed them and helped them back to their seats, a lady with blue hair began to play the piano banging out every chord. The congregation stood and sang with feeling and power until the walls fairly pulsated. Then it was time to ride the bus back home.

That afternoon, when the bus stopped in front of our home, Mother met us on the front porch.

"Well, girls, did you enjoy Sunday School?"

I shrugged, avoiding eye contact with Mother, "Sure. I guess so. It was fun."

The church bulletin we'd brought home noted an upcoming special evening service, and Mother asked if we'd like to attend. Anticipating another exciting sermon, we said *yes, we would.* Mother would go with us.

It was dusk when we arrived at the church that evening. The kerosene lamps around the room gave off pools of soft light. The heat of the summer day lingered in the building, and several open windows caught the cool evening air. As the congregation filled the church they warmly welcomed Mother into their fold. The preacher, wearing the same threadbare suit he'd worn on Sunday, greeted his flock, shaking hands and chatting as they entered and took their seats. Finally, he began the sermon, his voice barely more than a whisper. The congregation held its collective breath and leaned forward in their seats to hear his words. As if a dial slowly turned, his volume increased with each new thought, his message filled with threats of terrible consequences without repentance.

The congregation, hypnotized, punctuated his words with *Amens* and *Praise the Lords*! His face gleamed rivers of sweat. "Sinners! Yes, *you* sinners! You are doomed to hell's eternal fires! Save yourself tonight, join me up here and feel the power!"

Really rolling now he stripped off his suit jacket and slung it across the platform. With a shrug he yanked off his vest and tossed it after the jacket. With a frown firmly in place, Mother peered over her glasses to Pat, then to me. With raised eyebrows I shrugged indicating my surprise. She looked for a moment as if she would grab us by the hand and walk out.

The kerosene lamp, encircled by fluttering moths, hung but a few inches above his head. As his preaching intensified, his arms thrashed about, and we held our breath expecting him to strike the lamp. Empowered by his faith, he never did.

Pat and I, hunkered low in the pew, exchanged quick looks across Mother's lap wondering when the fun would start and folks would begin to fall to the floor. Sure enough, several of the congregation went forward. Some fell to the floor in the aisles. Others made it to the stage where they lay moaning. Mother sucked in her breath and pulled herself upright. She threw stiff glances at Pat and me, but we were absorbed in the spectacle.

Little was said on the ride home in the bus that evening, but that was the last time we attended the little church in the hills. I guess Mother felt we'd had enough religion to last until we could attend more serene worship. Many services attended over the years fade from memory, but those fiery sermons that hot summer long ago are laminated in my memory for all time.

Letting Down the Net

by Malone T. Davidson

Where the French Broad River turns,
a fly fisher flicks her rod
side-river towards the rocks
and undergrowth.

Her man-made waders swallow her
small frame, and she struggles
across the current
heading upstream.

Near the river, new souls go
under for three counts.
The chlorine burns their
tear filled eyes.

The waders-wearing preacher
pulls them up fresh and renewed
saying to the crowds, "Here is water;
what hinders you?"

Moving King's Creek

by Susan M. Lefler

How do you move a creek? I want to know.
Tell it sad stories bound to make it weep?
Do you sing to it, hoping you love
the same tunes—the kind you move to?
Perhaps, you sort of wave your hands,
like modern parents do, who never spank,
encouraging the banks to bend,
reshape the farmer's straight, sharp line.
You could depend on backhoes to invent
a path the little creek might want to go—
and once you settle on the route, how
do you ask the water in? How beckon
microscopic atomies, communities of fish?
Do you pack up and rearrange its stones?
What will the Great Blue Heron say,
who comes at 4 each day to dine?
Or the California lady, who dreamed
of Appalachian bottom land, worked
five years to reach it, only to find
they planned to leave her creekless?
I don't deny our creek could use a facelift,
banks caved in like mouths without their dentures.
I only ask if this cutting and pasting
of creeks might be extreme.
Another creek, in another aeon,
trimmed its labyrinthine way, layer
by layer, grandly carving gorges out.
Imagine God shouting: "Grab the backhoes, children.
We must divert this water course before it cuts too deep,
or we'll have us nothing but a Canyon here."
Where would we be then?
I only ask.

Antiques

by Estelle Darrow Rice

"Addie, I'm tired of sitting here every evening rocking and crocheting 'til the sun goes down, no offense to you." Maude dropped the doily she was crocheting for the church bazaar into the basket beside her chair.

"No offense taken, Maude. I'm tired of sitting here every evening too. You've made enough doilies for everyone in Valley Town."

"I 'speck so, but Brother Dawson always asks us to make 'em. Year after year. Year after year." Maude's chair creaked as she rocked back and forth. She stared down the winding road that meandered from their cabin on Stony Brook Mountain to the four-lane highway. "I always think of this old road leading away from our house rather than leading to it. If the wind blows just right, I can hear cars and trucks whizzing by, but no one ever stops."

The two women were silent for several minutes before Addie spoke.

"Maude, did you ever think we'd be a sitting here when we got old?"

"No."

"Neither did I. Life turned out kinda funny didn't it?"

"Nothing funny 'bout it."

Maude pushed the stray, gray hair out of her eyes. It had always been unruly even when it was chestnut brown. She took a white handkerchief with tatted trim out of her apron pocket and wiped her eyes. "I declare these old eyes don't see so good."

"Nothing to see anyway," Addie said. "Remember when my Rob used to drive up in his old Willis every Sunday afternoon all the way from Robbinsville. Said I was worth the drive. If I jumped up to meet him, Pa always said, "Sit down, Addie. It ain't seemly for a proper girl to run after no boy. Rob weren't no boy. He was a man, and I knew he was going to ask Pa for my hand."

"Addie, no use thinking back that far. We're still here and can't do much about it, even if we was of a mind to."

"Guess not," Addie said. She stood up and shuffled to the edge of the porch. She tucked her skirt behind her knees and sat on the top step. Her skirt draped in front of her legs almost to her shoes. "Mama always said, 'Keep your knees together and be ladylike.' I try to remember, but Maude, who are we trying to be ladylike for? Do you ever think about leaving here?"

"I used to, but I don't any more."

"Maude, I think about Rob lots. Do you think about Josh and Baby Betsy?"

"Course I do, but it makes me lonesome. I didn't expect to outlive both of them. She was a pretty little thing. When she laughed, it was like I imagine the angels sound."

Maude crocheted faster, bit the thread and tossed the finished doily on top of the others in her basket. "I want to take some jonquils to the cemetery Sunday." She twisted the thread with her needle and began another chain. "Addie, you could have married someone 'sides Rob."

"Didn't want to."

"Well, here we are two old ladies jawing about nothing we can change."

"I'm going to think of something. Maybe dream about it. I don't want to die a mean, lonesome, old woman."

"You're always conjuring up fancy ideas and look where we are— in the same house, on the same porch, living with the same old furniture Mama and Pa got when they was first married."

"Maude, I'm going inside now and go to bed. I want to start early on my dreaming. Don't stay up too late. The skeeters are big as horseflies tonight, and one might carry you off."

"If they could have they would have a long time ago," Maude said.

Addie let the screen door flap shut as she entered the house. Her iron bed was neatly made up with the double wedding ring quilt Rob's mother made long before Rob was killed in France. She gave it to Addie because it should have been a wedding present when Rob came home. But Rob came home in a box.

Addie thought she could dream better when the weather was cool enough to crawl beneath the old quilt's folds. It was cool most nights in the hills, so she did a lot of dreaming.

She smiled as she felt herself drifting off to sleep. The quilt was working its magic again. *There is a way to change our lives. We don't have to be stuck down this forsaken road the rest of our lives with only ourselves to talk to.*

When the rooster crowed at first dawn, Addie thought, *That old bird should 'a' been in a stew a long time ago, but he's too tough to be good eating. Besides he's still got a little spark and the hens like him.*

She threw back the quilt and without putting on her slippers she hurried into Maude's room. "Wake up. We've got a lot of work to do. Things are gonna change. Do we still have white paint left from fix'n up the house last year and a little of that trim paint?"

Maude rolled over and rubbed her eyes. "Paint? Whatever for?"

"I'll tell you later. Get up. We're gonna make this old place shine. You start making cookies, and I'll paint the sign."

"Cookies? Sign? Addie, what hair-brained scheme do you have now?"

Addie explained and Maude gasped. "What would Mama think about strangers using her things?"

"Ma and Pa ain't here no more. Maude, we've got to do something or we'll dry up."

Maude shook her head but followed her sister's instructions.

Addie brought the paint up from the barn and painted a sign as neatly as she could *ANTIQUES*. She dragged the sign to where the road met the four-lane and pounded it into the dirt with a rock. She returned to the house where Maude was resting on the porch.

"This is going to work, Maude. Everybody these days are looking for antiques."

"I don't feel right about this, Addie."

"You will. Wait and see."

Several hours later a car covered with dust from the country road stopped in front of the house. When Maude and Addie peeped through the curtains, they saw a man, a lady, and a small girl coming up the steps.

"I told you," Addie said and opened the door.

"We saw your sign and thought we'd come down to see your antiques," the woman said.

Addie grinned. "Come right in. My sister and I were getting ready to have some coffee and cookies. Please, have some with us. I'll bet the little lady would like a lemonade."

Addie and Maude led the family inside. They took out the ornate china their Ma saved for special occasions, put a plate of cookies on the table, and poured lemonade for the child and coffee for the adults.

After a polite length of time, the couple said the cookies were delicious. The man and woman looked at each other, then at the sisters who were sipping their coffee daintily. "We're enjoying the refreshments, but where are the antiques your sign advertised?"

"You're looking at 'em." Addie pointed to herself and to Maude. "Sorry to mislead you, but we certainly 'preciate you dropping by. It's mighty quiet up here with nobody but us to talk to. We hope you all will call again."

"Can we? Can we?" the little girl said.

The man laughed. "Sure. Glad to. This is the best antiquing trip I've ever had. I believe I hear more 'customers' coming down the road."

"Wonderful," Maude said. "Addie, we'd better get some more cookies."

Tomato Man

by Glenda Beall

Ruby tomatoes in small tan baskets
beg me to buy my lunch. Overalled
and raisin brown, he sits slumped
on the tailgate of a rusty red pickup,
his floppy hat a shade against the burning sun.

Will the two-dollar baskets buy him
groceries to take home to the waiting
wife who helped him pick the plump fruit?
Or will he go by Bernie's Quik Stop
for a six pack or two and cigarettes

that stain his teeth and tar his lungs?
He thanks me for my business,
but his faded eyes show
a mind that's somewhere else.
Today takes care of today. Tomorrow

he'll be here again, the tomatoes
redder, softer, with a few fresh ones
sprinkled in, to appeal to eyes of
passers-by, invisible people who
smile and speak, but never see him.

Woman in Red

by Brenda Kay Ledford

Look at Jezebel dressed
all in red trying
to beguile men like
the serpent deceived Eve.

Look at her sashaying
to the front. The back
pew's empty. Let her sit
there. It's good enough.

She's Baptist, you know.
Her dad preached brush arbors
and her mama's dirt poor.
What's she doing here?

There she goes tapping
down the aisle in red
spike heels. Deacon Puett
fell off the pew
staring at that woman in red.

Homecoming at Mt. Zion Baptist Church

by: Blanche L. Ledford

I was the only white person attending the homecoming at Mt. Zion Baptist Church slap in the middle of the black community of Texana. I'd always wanted to attend an African-American church and figured this was a good time. The country church was perched on a hill overlooking white businesses in Murphy, North Carolina. Probably the colored folks were shoved up there by the rich whites, but Texana is the prettiest part of town.

On this Sunday morning in September, the golden edges of poplar leaves glittered in liquid sunshine. A pocket of fog licked the gray marble courthouse of Murphy like a silver shawl, and purple clouds scratched the horizon. Mt. Zion stood on the hill like a beacon bidding weary lambs to come and rest a while in the sweet arms of Jesus.

When I entered the little church, I was warmly welcomed by an usher who grinned with his gums. He escorted me to the last empty pew in a sea of black faces. I felt odd being the only white in the congregation. Now I knew how minorities must feel. I noticed black praying hands on the communion table. I was surrounded by the beautiful color of black and realized that God is black, white, brown or red. He's no respecter of persons.

I never knew prejudice. I worked beside the blacks hoeing rows of corn during the Great Depression. They wore colorful head rags and sang as they beat weeds from the baked clay earth. They laughed, jived and made backbreaking work fun. I thought of the blacks as friends for they were my neighbors. I'd never heard of the colored sitting on the back seat of buses, because we had no transport system in the mountains of western North Carolina. We had no colored restrooms or separate facilities for the whites. Everyone used either the outhouse or the woods.

So I resent people who accuse southerners of being prejudiced. I'm proud of my heritage. Most of my family fought for the Confederate army during the Civil War. Uncle Eli marched barefoot to Pennsylvania and was killed in the Battle of Gettysburg. My grandfather tucked his tail and deserted the south. He dressed like a woman and hid in Matheson Cove until after the war.

I'm not proud of the fact that my great-grandparents owned slaves in Pickens County, Georgia. The 1860 inventory of the Townsend estate listed the value of slaves: Carolina and her infant child ...$1,450; Hannah was forty-six years old and cost $500; and Stephen was four-years-old and was listed at $450. Black males were appraised at $3,000 if they were young and healthy. Sadly, a bay mare was listed for $775, valued more than many human lives. Slavery was one of the greatest evils in American history. Had I lived then, and women allowed to vote, I would have voted for Abe Lincoln. I'm glad most of my family was too poor to own slaves. They were farmers who dug their living out of the dirt under the eye of a sizzling sun.

It was as hot as hoeing a cornfield in July in the packed church at Texana. I gasped for breath and wiped sweat from my forehead. The congregation thrashed the air with cardboard fans depicting Martin Luther King. A teenager flipped on the window air conditioner, and it was a taste of heaven. The deacon stood, pointed his finger, and yelled, "Don't you turn that thing on! It freezes my bones. Turn if off, I says." The boy ignored the old timer and shuffled out of the church muttering.

Next a little girl handed out bulletins to the congregation. She wore a charcoal polka dot dress and had a black bow in her braids. Her walnut-colored eyes sparkled as she grinned with pearly white teeth. She reminded me of my youngest child when she was 5-years-old. I never could control Brenda. She was like a wild colt all the time getting into something. One time she found my red, high-heeled shoes hid in the back of my closet. Someone gave them to me, but I never wore them because red was considered a sinful color by self-righteous church members. But that little lizard found my shoes and stomped through our shotgun house shouting like Lizzie Mae at church. Despite myself I giggled, and that made her show off even more, like a little monkey. She was a live-wire and still is as an adult.

I looked at the bulletin and was jarred back to the homecoming service at Texana. I couldn't believe it! Lunch would not be served until 3:00 p.m. How could I survive that long without food? I only had a piece of cinnamon toast and a glass of orange juice for breakfast. My stomach growled and I popped a Cert into my mouth because people were looking at me and grinning. I squirmed on the hard pew and wondered when the worship service would begin. Suddenly, someone thumped the piano and a procession of youth and senior choirs cut through the door. They clapped their hands and loudly sang, *Some glad morning when this life is o'er, I'll fly away...* The choir swayed in time with the lively music. I noticed each person had a different skin color. Some were dark as black pepper, others colored like cloves, some like nutmeg, and one lady was cinnamon.

The pastor spoke first. "I appreciate the ushers because they are the ones who welcome folks when they come into the church. I'm glad to see everyone here today, especially our white sister who's visiting us. I hope she won't get worn out before our service begins," he added with a chuckle. "The first lady and I appreciate very much everyone making this the best homecoming we've ever had at Mt. Zion Baptist Church."

The pastor's wife was called the first lady by the church members. She adjusted her flamboyant hat that had a huge black flower on the side and decorations like an octopus. Light reflected off the glass beads on her navy dress. She stood and gave her testimony.

"Well, a sister accused me of thinking I am better than others when I wear this hat. I've got news for you! I'm not better than anyone, but if you aren't saved, I'm better than you are. Four years ago I had an aneurysm of the brain and almost died. The Lord healed me. I'll fight anyone for him," she added with a laugh.

I did feel for the preacher's wife, what a nasty thing to say about her hat. I was also a pastor's wife for forty years. I wore a smile when I greeted the congregation, but bled inside. I had no freedom to be myself, to go where I pleased, to express my opinions, to have good clean fun. I made my clothes. If I bought a new dress people talked about me and said I was a spendthrift. I despised prune-faced women who lusted after my husband. He was good looking.

One woman, named Ann, grabbed my husband and gave him a bear hug in church. She dipped snuff and her teeth looked like she had eaten dirt. She ignored me as she made a high dive for my husband. After she slung her arms around his neck, she turned to me and smugly said, "I bet you can't hug him like that!" grinning with black teeth. I wanted to yank out her mousy hair, but I just smiled.

I had to take a lot of garbage off people. I couldn't even go to the grocery store without people poking their noses into my cart to see what I bought. If we had depended upon the church to feed us, we would have starved. My husband was a bi-vocational minister. He ran bulldozers during the week and was the pastor of several churches. Sometimes he got only $5.00 as a love offering. Some love! If preachers of today received so little pay, there would be a shortage in the ministry. The love of money is the root of all evil as the Good Book says. Oh, my goodness! Here they are passing the offering plates at the black church. I had only one dollar to give, my Social Security check being stretched to the limit.

After the first lady finished speaking, the visiting preacher, wearing a white robe, walked to the pulpit. He delivered a fire-and-brimstone message that burned for two hours. He pounded the pulpit with his fist, plopped down at the piano and slammed the keys with his back as he hollered, "Some of you is dragging. Get real about being Christians!" He stood, stomped the floor and flapped his arms like pelican wings. Sweat ran down his face and his robe looked like it had been dipped in Valley River. The congregation shouted, "Yes, sir! All right, Reverend!" A stooped, white-headed lady hopped up and danced in circles about the church. It was an emotional and lengthy service.

When we broke for lunch at 3:00, I wanted to run to the fellowship hall. I was weak with hunger pains. I got at the back of the line, but everyone insisted I go first. The tables were decorated with flowers, black napkins and plates. A feast was spread: green beans, chicken and dumplings, corn-on-the-cob, cornbread, mashed potatoes, black peas, hog jaw, grits, fried chicken, walnut cake, pecan pie, apple pies, banana pudding and many other dishes. It was so delicious that I got a second serving of food.

After lunch, afternoon service started at 4:00 p.m. It was a repeat of the morning service: more preaching, more shouting, more swaying, more clapping, more foot stomping, more thumping on the piano, more Negro spirituals: *Going to lay down my burdens, down by the riverside.* The singing was hypnotic and I started swaying like a pendulum in time with the mournful music. I dabbed tears that were splashing down my face as emotions churned in the little church. My spirit was lifted.

Service finally ended at 7:30 that evening. I stumbled out of the church with a paralyzed rear end after sitting all day on the hard pew. It was the longest and best service I had ever attended. The congregation warmly shook my hand and invited me to visit their church again. I just smiled. I'd had enough religion to last for a long, long time.

The Slipping

by Kenneth Chamlee

Migration is a cumbersome word
for monarchs slipping through Tunnel Gap.
Once he lay a whole day counting: they flickered
out of nothing, coasted
the hanging laurel, then dipped on Tiffany wings
into the blue-smoked valley. Maybe
a hundred, and time easily wasted.

He knows the monarchs rolled like cloudfire
forty years ago, burning toward milkweed
and the trembling Mexican forests
where they stay the winter or die.

September. He grabs his boots, drives the Parkway
to their crossing point. What is true
slips between the seasons, and nothing is louder
than the silent highways of rutted air and age.
And too many days, like today, he yields to each
unknowable need, drifting
as the monarchs straggle through.

Applebutter Time

by Joyce H. Foster

Pumpkins, untethered from their umbilical greenery,
sprawl across fields into roadside stands.
They scramble onto stoops and peer from windows
fluttering grins through snaggle teeth.

Bittersweet vines with bleary eyes
creep out of the woods onto trellises.
They wind around wreaths and slip into baskets
entwining wild corn and painted gourds.

In apple-scented houses fresh belles tease,
their flesh beckon to be touched, to be taken,
to be baked in crusts or caramelized,
to be chewed or stewed into velvety butter.

On market shelves the fruits of summer,
once shy buds that bulged into ripeness
then spilled into season,
now sit shriveling in their dotage.

The crone nudges me with her weathered broom
and warns that winter snow is near
when white skin will sag from gnarled limbs
splayed like ghosts against the night.

Warned of my withering string of days
I long to toss my tepid life
into her boiling cauldron
and swirl in spices and cupfuls of sugar.

I want to hold my heart over the open flame
and hoard each passionate flicker
that I might savor the warmth
when the quivering time arrives.

Bear With Us

by Doug Woodward

It was an eye opener. Nobody could argue with that. Like Pearl said, "Nothing like this has *ever* happened in our valley! Even Pink's snakebite couldn't hold a candle to the ruckus Essie's run caused."

For those of you who might not remember, Pink was sitting in his rocker on the front porch of his cabin when he was bitten on the hand by a flying snake head. It seems his grandson was mowing the yard when he spotted the copperhead and with great glee shredded it on his next pass. Pink's hand was stiff as a board for two months, but other than being a little more ornery than usual, he seemed to have undergone no ill effects. The snake could not make the same claim.

Essie had caused a bit of a stir when she moved to the settlement. She had bought Zeb's cabin up in the cove which included ten acres of mountain hardwoods that backed up to government land.

"Taint no place for a lone lady," Texas had said. "Livin' that far back, she needs a man to take care of matters."

But that was five years ago. Esther Mae Patton had proved them all wrong. She appeared able to handle any challenge that mountain living might bring. At least, until that fateful Sunday morning.

Zeb's cabin was rather stark and not long on amenities, but it was well placed to catch the winter sun. The early settlers knew what they were doing when it came to passive solar, even if they didn't call it by that name. Essie had made some changes, not the least of which was bringing the plumbing indoors. A spring, higher up the mountain, provided gravity-water, and Essie had rigged up an old water heater tank, coils of black pipe and a glass covered box to provide plenty of hot water, courtesy of the sun.

The cabin had small windows and tended to be dark inside, so when she replaced the cedar shakes on the roof, Essie installed two large skylights to brighten up the place.

"She's a right handy lady, she is," Texas had to admit when he hauled the cast-iron bathtub up the mountain in his pickup and helped her wrestle it into place beneath one of the skylights. Essie had just finished splitting nearly two cords of firewood that morning.

Even though the community grudgingly had to admit that Essie seemed to know what she was doing, she remained, in their view, a pretty strange character. As a writer, she spent many hours alone at her cabin and, to her neighbors, seemed to have no visible source of income. This alone was enough to generate strange rumors.

That was not all. She had gently but firmly declined several invitations to the Cold Spring Baptist Church even though the church was only half a mile down the road, the closest place to hers. Essie had given no hint of her own faith or affiliation, and Annie Nell had confided to several of her friends in the local homemakers group, "I just *know* she's one of those *New Agers*! And what's more, she doesn't eat meat!"

But they had to admit, at age forty-three, Essie was in much better shape than any of her critics. More than once, Annie Nell's husband, Hiram, had nearly put the tractor in the ditch while watching Essie pass by on her morning run down the valley. She usually ran early, and this was particularly important on Sundays, since she had to go right past the church and didn't wish to offend any of her neighbors.

It was September and high canning season for most of the settlement. Essie had put by almost four dozen quarts of beans and had also made applesauce from the apples in Zeb's old orchard. On the cabin roof, she had rigged up a solar drier for thin apple slices, covered with a layer of cheesecloth to discourage thieving birds.

For Brimstone, a 600 pound black bear in her fifth autumn, it had not been a good year. Her son, Quicknose, now two, had left to follow his own pursuits, and she had been without cubs for two seasons. A development called Harmony Grove had been built smack in the middle of what was once her favorite blueberry patch, and this fall's acorn crop was the sparsest in thirty years.

Thus it was that Brimstone's hunger drew her down the mountain to Essie's cove. At first it was the small orchard that attracted her attention, but she soon found there were no apples left within easy reach. Even so, her keen nose told her that there must be more nearby, and she lumbered toward the cabin to investigate. It took but a few moments to shinny up the white oak and gingerly transfer her weight to the cabin roof where the sliced apples were drying. The pitch of the roof where Brimstone made this first transition was fairly gentle. However, the roof slope where the apples were drying became considerably steeper, and it was here that she lost it. As her claws ripped out of the shakes, Brimstone made a last futile lunge for the apples but instead took a tumbling plunge down the roof.

Essie was pleased with herself. It was a fine Sunday morning, the air was cool, and her run had been exceptionally fast. She kicked off her running shoes, popped a Lorena McKennett CD into the stereo and drew a tubfull of water. The water in the tub was a bit too hot, so she went to the kitchen for a bowl of granola while she anticipated the relaxing soak.

Slipping out of her running outfit, Essie tossed it into the hamper and grabbed a fresh towel. She pushed aside the door curtain to the bathroom and took one step inside. It was at this moment that Brimstone also entered the bathroom.

When a 600 pound bear bursts through your skylight in a shower of glass and ends up in the bath you were about to enjoy, it takes a moment to grasp the situation. But not many moments. As Brimstone stood up in the tub with a bellow and looked Essie in the eye, the decision was immediate. Essie dropped the towel and was outta there. And from Brimstone's point of view? Well, when you've just taken an unexpected fall, cut your foot and find yourself in hot water, you might be inclined to blame present company!

Brimstone made a lunge for Essie, slipped on the edge of the tub and ended up with one hind leg caught in the commode. With a roar of frustration, she tried to disengage, and ended up ripping the toilet out of its moorings. This gave Essie just the lead she needed. She was through the cabin door and down the road like a shot, Brimstone a hundred feet behind. They were pretty evenly matched, what with Brimstone having a one-toilet handicap!

Some say that Essie set a new Olympic record for the 800 meter run that day, and if Hiram had been on his tractor, he would have dropped his eyeballs. But when Deacon Birch looked up and saw Essie approaching, it was not her running that was on his mind! He was about to shout to the parson that *now* something had to be done about this outrageous lady, but he didn't have time. He suddenly realized Essie wasn't running *past* the church, she was running *in it!*

"Don't look!" screamed Mattie Sue as she clapped a hand over her husband, Sam's, eyes. The fact that they were still underway in the church parking lot didn't really register until their Chevy came to rest ten yards inside the graveyard.

The early teen Sunday schoolers were just finishing up in the vestibule. "Even your innermost thoughts cannot be hidden. We all stand naked before the Lord," the teacher admonished. As Essie burst through the front doors, the class self-destructed.

About this time, Brimstone rounded the corner, still sporting the toilet. Texas had just eased his pickup into the lot, took one look, and reached for his gun rack. "You can't!" gasped his wife, "It's Sunday, we're at church, and it's not even bear season yet!"

"The hell I can't," growled Texas. "This is self defense!" He squeezed off a round from the 30-06.

Fortunately for Brimstone, the shot hit squarely on the commode, shattering it in a hundred pieces. Suddenly free, she accelerated to top speed, bursting through the barbed wire of the Bradley pasture, scattering cows in all directions. This act probably saved her life, as Texas couldn't get off another shot without endangering his neighbor's livelihood. As for Brimstone, she had already decided it was her last visit to Cold Spring Valley.

Deacon Birch and Parson Savage were frozen like a pillar of salt. It was Sidney Jane, the choir director, who saved the moment, snatching a spare robe from the choir closet and tossing it to Essie whose awareness was just now catching up with her body.

Some late arrivals that morning said they had never heard the choir sing so sweetly and the new voice added a lot. Parson Savage always regretted not having seized the moment for an on-the-spot baptism. The Bryson boys, who had never before seen a naked woman anywhere, regarded it as answered prayer.

As for Essie, she built an indoor dehydrator that week.

Postscript: *While I was away biking and photographing grizzlies in Alaska, a large black bear visited our home in North Carolina for four days in a row, watching the kids through the picture windows on ground level and nosing around the residue of apple butter making, which had been dumped near the front deck. When I later got on the roof to clean the chimneys, I found that the bear had been there too. She had stepped off the mountain onto the bathroom roof, which has a gentle pitch, and torn out several shakes near the large skylight which is directly above our bathtub. For some reason she had climbed from there to the steeper part of the roof and made it almost to the ridge. But at that point she slipped and left deep claw marks for about ten feet down the shakes, to a point where she must have either somersaulted or rolled the rest of the way. Envisioning "what might have happened" gave birth to this bit of fiction!*

The Sentinel

by Helen N. Crisp

A lone cornstalk stands in the field,
Over at the edge, near the fence.
The ground is cleared, turned under for winter.
It is time for the earth to rest,
a time to renew for the year ahead.
The two ears of corn on the stalk
are being picked clean by the crows.

This lonely sentinel watches over nothing.
Nothing moves. There is nothing to see.
The rest and rebirth cannot be heard.
When spring comes he, too, will be gone.
He'll be plowed under if he is still standing.
Maybe he will fall to the ground this winter and rot.

Corn will grow in the field again,
but not from this seed.

Of Possums and Pumpkin Wine

by Connie Quinn

Poppy was both overjoyed and unsettled by the news in his sister's letter. Carefully folding the pencil-written page, he put it in the pocket of his old woolen coat, pulled the toboggan cap down tightly on his head and started down the rough dirt road toward home. It seemed that May's husband, Tom, was thinking about taking a job in Asheville, so she had decided to pay a visit on their way up to take a look at the area. Apparently, the letter had been delayed because she was due to arrive the next day. There was little time to prepare. Poppy was glad that the children were visiting Uncle John's family and would not be there requiring attention.

As he passed by the smokehouse, he selected a nice string of fresh leather britches beans and a piece of ham. Early in the morning, he would pick some greens, grind corn for meal, and set sweet taters by the hearth to roast.

Scurrying up the shaky, plank steps, he let the screen door slam and rattle behind him as he rushed to tell his wife, Bessie, the news. He found her stoking the wood stove to cook a pot of hash and some cornbread. New cakes of rich, hard butter surrounded the butter mold and quart jars of fresh milk sat ready to go to the spring house. He was pleased to think how much May would enjoy a real country supper. However, his troubled thoughts kept going back to the one problem that was nagging at him. What was he going to do about the still?

When he had meticulously built it in the kitchen, behind the wood cook stove, he had been satisfied that it was a place safe from prying eyes. It never occurred to him that he might, sometime, want to hide it from his own kin. What was he going to do?

Though his moonshining had never been proven, Poppy had been the object of conversation for years. And when a mysterious fire burned a meeting place of the Church of God, he was among twenty men questioned. None were found responsible for the fire. Still he had a somewhat checkered past. The local gossips had gotten good mileage out of him, and it had been hard to live down. May honestly believed that Poppy had reformed his ways, and that still would be a sore disappointment to her.

While Bessie went about fixing supper, Poppy got a Mason jar, drew off a sample of his current run of shine, and shook it to test for quality. Instantly the clear liquid was swirling with the beads that heralded a good batch. After putting it into jars, he tossed the last few dregs toward the fire. Before they reached the flames, they exploded into bursts of blue fire and vanished. Yes, he thought, this was a very good run and would bring top dollar from those upstanding men in town who sneaked off to have a snoot-full.

The government and the holier-than-thou locals didn't understand that making a little hooch was the difference in having money to buy a new coat and some shoes for the children, or to see them with rags wrapped around their feet. Times were hard for people high up in the North Carolina mountains. Equally frustrating, he thought as he walked toward the shed, were the folks who were critics of shine but seemed to accept a little homemade wine. Very likely they overlooked the wine because they drank it themselves.

With the Mason jars carefully hidden, he turned his attention to the pumpkins and their on-going fermentation. After lifting the cloths and removing the stem plugs, he poured more sugar inside the rinds. It wouldn't be long until the pumpkins dissolved and the wine would be ready to bottle and age.

Big Boy, his pet possum, waddled over to sniff around to see if Poppy had something for him. He was rewarded with a ride on Poppy's shoulder down to the spring-house where they both enjoyed a ripe apple. Poppy had rescued and raised many such orphaned possums through the years, releasing them outside the back door when they were ready to fend for themselves. Thus, he had many nightly visitors who came inside through the cat hole. Nor was it uncommon to find possums gone to bed somewhere in the house. Bessie, knowing Poppy's love and understanding of nature, accepted his Cherokee belief that all creatures were his brothers and sisters in life's journey.

Poppy's musings were disturbed when Bessie pulled the cord at the back door of the house, clanging the bell at the spring-house. It was time to eat. The steaming hash and cornbread buffered them against the cold in the old, creaking house. After supper, they straightened the house by the dim light of kerosene lanterns. There was really not much to tidy up because they had but a few possessions. They talked about the still, wondering what they would do. It seemed that the best they could do was to keep May out of the kitchen.

The fateful morning arrived. Poppy hung quilts on the clothesline behind the house in an attempt to hide the still's smoke hole and hoped for the best. Bessie cooked the leather britches, ham, greens and cornbread, and she set out the fresh butter and milk. Tom and May arrived at three o'clock.

Poppy hurried out, met his sister at the edge of the road, and gave her a bone-creaking bear hug. Pausing on the old wooden footbridge, they looked for minnows and watched the creek rush around the mossy rocks. Arm in arm they passed beneath a brightly colored canopy of hickory trees that lined the old pathway to the house. Laughing and kicking at leaves, May picked up acorns from the tree that Poppy liked to climb and hide in when he wanted to aggravate Bessie. May shined the acorns and stuck them in her pocket.

Supper was soon ready, and May explained that she was sorry they'd have to eat and rush off, but the car had broken down outside Chattanooga and they wanted to get on to Asheville in case they had more trouble. Tom seated himself in front of the warm morning heater to read the newspaper, but May, hungry for country cooking, helped herself to the vittles. While May ate, Bessie recounted stories of the antics of Poppy and his animals. Bessie told May that on cold mornings they could be assured of finding possums in the bed covers.

"Poppy would have made a fine animal doctor," Bessie said.

When she finished eating, Poppy brought a cup of the pumpkin wine, for May to taste. "You're not moonshining are you, Brother?" Poppy tried to look innocent.

"Oh, you should have seen the pumpkins we raised this year. Some must have weighed fifty pounds, and most all flesh! Made some of the finest wine I've ever had! I'll get some for you to take along," he said as he hurried from the room to discourage May from following him to the kitchen.

When Poppy came back, Big Boy was riding on his shoulder, the scaly tail curled around Poppy's neck holding himself steady while he strained to grab for Poppy's big Mason jar of pumpkin wine.

"See, even Big Boy knows the good stuff," Poppy laughed.

Amid tears of farewell, May accepted the wine and a poke full of shuck beans and late tomatoes. She pined at the distance between them as Poppy walked her to the car where there was much hugging and tear drying. When she finally got settled, the car pulled away as Poppy called after them, "Come again, one and all."

After watching the car disappear down the hollow, Poppy turned slowly toward the house. He was happy to have seen May, sad that their time together was so short, but relieved that she had not seen the still. By the time he and Bessie picked up the table and washed the dishes with the last of the hot water from the stovetop, it was dark and they were both worn out.

The night sky was moonlit, deep, and starry. With no breeze stirring, the rapidly dropping temperature promised a hard freeze. Since there was no electricity in the mountains at that time, Poppy always let the fire die down until the wood was glowing red logs of hot ash and then banked the fire by covering it with white, dusty, burned-out ashes. Meanwhile, Bessie took the little clothes irons from the hearth, wrapped them in flour sacks, and put them in the bed to help warm their feet. Then, with Bessie in her long, wool, flannel gown, and Poppy in his wool long-handles, they settled down to warmth and rest.

Sometime in the early morning hours, Poppy was awakened by the movement of some of Big Boy's children under the mounds of quilts and blankets. He pulled his wool toboggan over his ears and watched his breath in the cold stillness. Poppy thought of how grateful he was that May had visited and that he had escaped her wrath for his impropriety. Then, right beside the bed there was a soft *clunk* and some rapid smacking sounds. Big Boy had turned over a jar of pumpkin wine, and was having a snort.

With an impish smile of boy-like satisfaction, Poppy drifted off to sleep muttering, "What May don't know won't hurt her!"

Log Cabin Get Together

by Linda M. Smith

Four boars' heads look down on me,
with upturned tusks they smile.
Black bear wears a red sombrero.
He looks happy too.
Ten point buck wears a gray cap
with picture of a gun, says I don't call 911.
Bobcat on hind feet paws at
Elvis on black velvet.

Dream catchers, blue feathers and beads
hang above the counter,
piled high with 'gator tail, fried crispy,
(the friend from Florida brought),
bear meat, biscuits and soup beans,
taters, ramps and slaw.

Women around the table pare
and cut for apple butter.
"Randy's looking for a woman."
"What happened to Dianne?"
"She left him for another man."
"But *he* bought her a car."

Guys around the bonfire
drink beer or shine and laugh.
Fire dims, "getting cool, let's go in."
Guitars come out with mandolin.
Fiddles and blues harp play
"Rocky Top Tennessee."

Moon is rising over Snowbird.
"It's time to go back home."
We drive the dark, black road
with our bellies full.
Even the moon is smiling.

Climbing Mountains

by Richard Argo

This wasn't a bicycle ride, it was a pilgrimage. Like Tibetan monks or ancient Incas, bicyclists, dressed in shirts and shorts of optic orange, yellow and green, trudged up the right side of the road, pushing their bikes by hand. Like penitents they marched toward the Holy Grail that was the Blue Ridge Parkway and Pisgah Mountain. Their multicolored biking helmets bobbed, free arms swung and legs stepped in a rippling unison until they looked like a huge caterpillar crawling up the road. The pedal clips on the bottom of their biking shoes, those metal and plastic devices that snap into the fig newton sized pedals, clicked as they walked on pavement, like baseball cleats on concrete. I think they liked to hear that sound, but it made me want to shout, "Hey, if you were going to walk up this mountain, why did you wear those silly shoes?"

It was Tuesday, October 5, 1999, the third day of the inaugural Murphy to Manteo bicycle tour, a two week, 720 mile tour that meandered across North Carolina from the mountains to the sea.

I left Brevard around seven-thirty that damp and hazy morning and followed the course along US 276, past the photo opportunity at Looking Glass Falls and into the Cradle of Forestry, where the CCC camps were started seventy odd years ago. It was nearly 9:00 a.m. when sunlight broke through clouds and filtered through the trees. The road began to rise toward the fourth major climb in three days and bicyclists came off their bikes like cowboys dismounting after a cattle drive. Now they trailed up the side of the road or sat in clusters, sucked on water bottles and ate nutrition bars. They looked like refugees. "Hey!" I thought, "If you were going to walk up this mountain, why bring bikes?"

Cycle North Carolina, with the cooperation of North Carolina Amateur Sports and the North Carolina Department of Transportation, conducted the tour. It was fully supported with on-course rest stops, SAG vehicles and mechanical assistance. There was a meal plan, provisions for indoor or outdoor camping, luggage transportation, evening shuttles to restaurants, stores or laundry and even nightly entertainment. But the focus of the tour was a daily, fifty to sixty mile, bicycle ride and, from the beginning, talk of the climbs dominated conversation. People came from all over the country to do this tour.

None expected to slam into these mountains like the coyote in a "Road Runner" cartoon. The reactions were all the same: "I've never seen anything like this." "Bike the Rockies wasn't this bad." "I'm from Iowa. How do I train for this?"

Arguments raged on which climb was worst: Junaluska Gap, the long grinding climb that wasn't too steep, but went on forever, or the short, sharp wall between Franklin and Lake Thorpe. Many riders could tell only by the sound of the strain on the SAG van's engine. That's how they finished the climb. They rode to the top in air conditioned comfort.

I remembered the first day of the tour, talking to Laverna as we climbed Wayah Crest. I had overtaken her a mile or so from the top. As I passed I asked how she was doing.

"How much farther?" she asked and struggled to keep her bicycle going.

It's hard to gauge people when they are beneath a helmet, sunglasses and riding togs, but from what I could see, she was at least a senior citizen.

"I don't know," I answered, and wished I could be more helpful. "Shouldn't be much longer."

"I think I'm going to stop," she said.

I glanced at the name and address card strapped to the cross bar of her bicycle, the tour's equivalent to stick-on name tags.

"Now, just where is Matthews, North Carolina?" I asked, hoping to take her mind off the climb.

She told me that it was outside Charlotte and for a while my ploy worked. We talked of many things from bicycle gears to grandchildren as we ground our way up the mountain. Finally, she said, "I'm going to stop."

And she did.

I went on to discover that we were only about a quarter mile from the top and I was disappointed that she had been so close and quit, until I heard later that Laverna from Matthews was, at eighty-six years, the oldest rider on the tour. Hey! At eighty-six, you're allowed.

Actually, all the riders were doing just what the tour director told us to do. "If the climb gets too hard, stop," he said. "This is a two week tour. No sense killing yourself in two days." Besides, these people had paid their money. If they wanted to walk from Murphy to Manteo, that was their business.

I may have been a rookie on this tour, but these mountains were my territory and I had other ideas. Maybe it was because I do most of my biking in western North Carolina where you either push up hill or glide down. Maybe it's because I bike alone and use these hills as a challenge.

Whatever the reason, for me, it's personal. Once I start a climb, barring a massive coronary, I will not stop before I reach the top.

My philosophy is this: the mountain can get no higher, no longer, no steeper. Its only weapon is patience. It just sits there. But every time I round a hairpin curve and see the road still ascending, the mountain whispers, "I'm still here." If the mountain's only weapon is patience, then that must be my weapon, too. For me to attack the mountain and try to push to the top as fast as I can, means failure. It's not about time; it's not about speed. It's about gearing down into the low range and grinding it out.

I followed a rider up the ledge between Franklin and Lake Thorpe until he dismounted and began to walk. Slowly, I pushed past him. After several minutes, I peeked around and the man was still right behind me. He was going almost as fast as I, but I was still on the pedals.

The circumference of a bicycle wheel is approximately seven feet. So every time the wheels make one revolution, the bike travels seven feet. That's how I make it to the top: seven feet, by seven feet, by seven feet. And when I round a hairpin turn and see the road ascending, when the mountain whisper's, "I'm still here," I whisper back, "So am I."

Picture Window

by Ralph Montee

Evenings we sit in front of the big window,
gaze at these mountains, seeing
little Drakensbergs or small Himalayas,
wave upon wave
moving over the dark and red earth,
remembering other mountains
we have come from
to these North Carolina mountains
we now call home.

Smiling, we recall the story that
Adam left his footprint
on the tallest mountain in Taprobane;
the Egyptians, lacking mountains
made them out of mud and stone.
Even New Yorkers set glass and steel towers
on flat Manhattan Island
to claim mountains of their own.

Our window's magic lantern
conveys us to places we have lived,
brings back old friends
we may not visit any other way.
While we yearn for them
as the riches of a lifetime,
we tend raspberries and beans,
pull weeds, feed birds, take care
of the neighbor's calico cat in winter,
climb new mountains, make new friends,
find another kind of richness here.

51

Shuufti

by Pat Montee

Sometimes I was glad to see him, but other times when I opened the door and saw him standing there I wished that I had looked out the window first. Then I would have seen his big, blue motorcycle standing out by the gate. It was unmistakably his, with the multi-colored woolen saddle bags hanging over the back, bulging with copper pots and trays, rolled prayer rugs, and heaven only knew what. No one else in Amman rode a motorcycle like that.

Then I could have ignored the doorbell and stood quietly at the back of the house pretending to be absent. Knowing him, however, he would have continued his vigorous jabbing of the door bell, sensing my presence in the same way he so often sensed my top price.

I can see us now. I open the door and find him standing there grinning pleasantly, displaying several gold teeth above an unshaven jaw.

"Marhaba, Madam!" he booms in a throaty baritone.

"Marhabteen, Shuufti." We shake hands. His clothes, a drab gray windbreaker over an ordinary shirt and trousers, are a nondescript contrast to the exotic articles he sells.

"Good, good things today, Madam! Good, good embroidery like you wanted last time; very special, Madam. You look. I know you like!"

There is a hint of vulnerability in his stance, despite the massive square shoulders. At this point I can still say, "Not today, Shuufti. Come another time." But somehow his posture pleads with me not to do that. Once past this stage, he will be in safe waters. From here on he can maneuver me, novice bargainer that I am, still smug in the delusion that I can divine from his starting price what the real price should be. But first he has to get past the door.

All too often I am a pushover. I really do like to see what he has wrapped in all the various cloths and plastic bags, one inside the other in ever-unfolding abundance.

"Well, OK. But no money today. Just look!"

"OK, Madam, OK. Just look!" And off he bounds down the steps to unfasten the camel saddle bags and hoist them over one shoulder while I stand watching. The speed with which he comes back in through the doorway belies the weight of the bags. I have seen him pull forth from their depths an enormous, copper, water urn that alone must have weighed thirty pounds.

It was always a lighthearted moment for us both, this entrance. He, fresh on the threshold of an opportunity for profit, and I, about to see a new array of treasures, possibly even acquire one.

It didn't matter that his announced purpose had been to show Palestinian embroidery pieces. Everything else in the bags was brought out too, carefully unwrapped and arranged around the living room. Shuufti had a good eye for the complementary background. Besides the embroidery, there might be Maria Theresa medallions from Jerusalem or heavy silver necklaces from Yemen. Sometimes copper pots he identified as Persian looked exactly like modern Syrian pots I had seen in Damascus. But I didn't hold him to truth in his presentations, any more than he did me as to how many dinars I actually did have to spend.

Shuufti was a nickname coined by his customers, most of whom were foreign housewives like myself. We called him Shuufti in good humored self-defense. It was a word he assailed us with constantly. The Arabic word shuuf, to look, becomes shuufti when addressed to a woman.

"Shuufti, Madam, shuufti. Here! You not find one like this any more!"

Shuufti was not one to let a product speak for itself. His hard-driving bargaining had earned him another nickname. The more cynical of his customers referred to him as Shifty. He was a frequent topic of conversation among Amman's foreign community.

"What's Shifty asking for that old Omani coffee pot these days?" we'd ask each other tentatively. He played deftly with our egos. His favorite response to a cry of pain over a price would be to point out that this was a very special price indeed – last week the wife of the Spanish Ambassador had paid twice that for one not so good as this one!

His real name was Abu Abid, father of Abid. He had several other children in addition to Abid. But, as is the Arab custom, he was called by the name of his firstborn son who was then eighteen.

His scruffy appearance made him an unlikely connoisseur. Usually his fingers were blackened from removing layers of tarnish from old metal pieces he purchased. Sometimes the layers were so heavy he used battery acid. But connoisseur he was. His wares were several cuts above those of the tourist shops in town.

He had no shop himself but instead traveled to his customers. The motorcycle and saddle bags were typical of the good sense he brought to his enterprise. He also wore a shiny modern motorcycle helmet. Even in Amman's rainy winter weather he could continue to conduct his portable business, wrapping everything well in the commodious woolen bags.

Shuufti had moved to Amman years before from a village near Hebron on the West Bank where he had traded in antiquities and village crafts for many years. Most of his best embroidery pieces came from there and from Gaza. In Amman much of his purchasing was from Muslim pilgrims on their way south to Mecca from Turkey or Syria or from Iraq across the Eastern desert. For many pilgrims this haj was a once-in-a-lifetime trip; and a common way of financing it was to sell household heirlooms along the way.

The eye-catching saddle bags weren't his only "PR". He had devised his own unique marketing method. He would invite a customer and family to come to his house for chicken Musakhan, a traditional Palestinian dinner dish. "And, please, bring your friends!"

Having previously stopped by to get a total of the number of guests to be expected, Shuufti arrived on time at the customer's home on the appointed evening. Motorcycle reflectors and helmet gleaming in the headlights, he guided the cavalcade to his house which was located in a maze of winding streets near one of the refugee camps across town. From the outside, the house was indistinguishable from its neighbors' cement block structures, flat roofs, and dusty door yards. Inside the resemblance ended. Here, three rooms were stacked from bare cement floor to ceiling with copper and brass trays, jugs, platters, pitchers, coffee pots, urns and samovars. Rugs spilled over from a pile which filled a small anteroom and lamps and woven saddle bags hung from ceiling rafters. There were gleaming surfaces and dull; fine quality and poor mingled together in careless profusion. These were rooms to be edged through slowly.

Shuufti's pleasant-faced wife stood in one doorway to be introduced. A softly spoken "Ahlan w sahlan,"–welcome twice welcome before she disappeared to continue work in the small kitchen. Deliciously pungent cooking aromas already drifted through the rooms.

The dining room for these occasions was a bedroom where the big double bed could seat a minimum of four. And there were also straight-backed wooden kitchen chairs.

But no one sat for long. This was the room in which Shuufti kept his most valuable pieces. The walls were covered with festoons of heavy silver and amber jewelry, daggers and swords. And the cabinets and drawers below were literally stuffed with more jewelry, Korans, trinkets and old pistols. In the gracious interlude before dinner Shuufti was the genial host. He kept busy answering questions and pulling out more treasures from the dark recesses of those bounteous shelves. Soon guests were browsing back through the other crowded rooms. Above muffled murmurs and the periodic clatter of dislodged brass, the kitchen radio played Arabic music. Shuufti's family stayed in the kitchen while a huge color TV sat dark in the bedroom amongst the guests. Dinner was simple and delicious: chicken baked with onions and spices, chopped fresh tomatoes and hot Arab bread.

When the tiny decorative cups for after-dinner coffee were at last replaced on the brass tray, business began. By this time most of Shuufti's guests would have spotted something to haggle for.

"Say, Shuufti, how much did you want for that copper lamp?" someone would begin, hoping the price quoted earlier in the evening might be different now. But it was a futile hope. Whether hours or weeks passed, Shuufiti never forgot a price.

"Fifteen JD (Jordanian dinar) ! Very good lamp! Too much? No, no, not too much. Look, look, Mister, see how strong here! Fifteen JD good price!"

A counter offer might wait while the next guest was attended to. I watched bemused at how many transactions Shuufti kept track of simultaneously, leaving one at mid-point to turn to another. Without a calculator, he could haggle in dollars or Sterling pounds or dinars at a dizzying pace.

Deals with new guests were seldom finalized that evening. Instead, subsequent trips by Shuufti to guests' homes were promised (at which time the saddle bags would contain tempting additional pieces). By the time the evening was over, jovial thanks and goodnights from the porch had to be said softly because neighbors' lights were already out and his family long since asleep.

Not long after one such evening I learned something surprising from a friend who had known Shuufti for many years. She began by asking if I had noticed (as I had) that when given a new name and address for a potential customer, Shuufti paid no attention to the proffered map or written directions. But he listened intently and insisted upon repeating the verbal information. This was because, she continued, he was illiterate in both English and Arabic.

When I knew I'd be leaving Amman I began to remind Shuufti of his promise to repair the hole in an old copper water jug he'd sold me.

"Maalish, Madam. Don't worry. I fix!"

It became a small chorus accompanying our encounters:

"Say, Shuufti, that copper..."

"Ah!, Yes! Not forget. Next time I bring things to fix."

As time grew short I hinted at new customer names I could give him and he told me he was searching for better solder.

"Will be fine. You like - I know!"

We live in the mountains of western North Carolina now. Our road is so steep even Jehovah's Witnesses seldom ring the doorbell. Some days I miss Shuufti's visits. But, in truth, something of his presence is here. Our days are still warmed by the blazing orange and dark reds of a woven kilim that once traveled in Shuufti's saddle bags, by an old brass coffee pot, and by the graceful curved lines of a leaky copper water jug.

The last time I saw Shuufti was in Amman traffic. He was speeding along on his motorcycle toward one of the new subdivisions outside town. I like to think he is ringing someone's doorbell right now. Maybe one of those names I gave him.

P.B.

by Ila Yount

P. B. became a part of our family some seventeen years ago. He was a grey and yellow cockatiel with two bright orange circles on his cheeks. He appeared one afternoon on the playground at the day-care where I worked. He simply flew down and landed in the midst of the children who were waiting for their parents to pick them up. We first became aware of him when we heard squeals from the children as he climbed from one lap to another. I picked him up, and he climbed on my shoulder and sat there very contentedly as I drove home.

We had a parakeet too, so after scrounging up one of his old cages, we put Pretty Bird in the cage, and he seemed perfectly content. For about six weeks, we ran an ad in the local paper trying to find his owner. We had numerous offers to take him, but none that claimed ownership. Weeks turned into months and months into years and he became a part of our family.

We were unaware that he could talk until one day when my daughter-in-law picked up his cage and he gave a loud wolf whistle. She was so startled that she almost dropped him. After that he began showing off his vocabulary. His favorite expression was, "You're a pretty bird," so we named him Pretty Bird and shortened that to P. B. He would really perk up if you whistled around him, and he learned to imitate the opening whistling of the Andy Griffin Show.

His wolf whistle almost got my husband in trouble one day. It was summertime and I had put P. B. out on the carport. My husband was asleep in a lounge chair, and a young woman was walking up the street. P.B. emitted his piercing whistle, she turned and looked to see who was whistling at her, and I suppose since she didn't see anyone but my husband, presumed it was he. Fortunately I looked out the door just as P.B. gave another whistle. The young woman turned and started toward my husband with a look of righteous indignation on her face. I hastily went out and rescued my husband and explained to her it was the bird that was whistling.

Our parakeet, that had never said anything, soon picked up most of P. B.'s expressions and they talked incessantly to each other. He also imitated the birdcalls he heard, which was very pleasant until he started imitating the blue jays. Then we had to cover his cage to get him to shut up.

P. B. died this week. He had stopped talking for the last two weeks. My son had taken him to the veterinarian to have his toenails clipped. The trauma of leaving the house may have caused him to be sick. The vet said he may have had a heart attack or an upper respiratory problem. Whatever it was, my house is too quiet now. I depended on him to let me know when someone came to the door and to say good night to me when I turned off the light at night. I miss P.B., my pretty bird.

Eagle's Nest

by Al Manning

Each morning as I come down off the ridge and turn the corner, there she is, looming in her majesty, the old mountain called Eagle's Nest. She is not a champion as mountains go. There are many in the Smokies of greater height. But those are dark and mysterious, isolated in the wilderness areas, to be approached and conquered only by an organized assault. She sits comfortably on the edge of the valley, her foothills sprawling out over the bottom land, much like a drowsy old hen that has fluffed out her feathers and settled down on her nest.

She is an old lady of many moods–now flighty as squirrels playing tag through the trees, then serene as a swan on a mill pond. In fall, she is a patchwork of gold, red and orange, a tattered clown suit splattered with paint. In dead of winter she is staid and dowdy, a landscape of but a single hue, predictable as the tick of a schoolhouse clock. During spring and summer, as clouds drift across the sun, their shadows race along her ramparts, the colors shifting and changing, now seen and then gone, impossible to remember yet never forgotten.

As winter cold fronts move in, and the cloud ceiling descends, sometimes I can see only her lower slopes, her tops remaining hidden in the mists. Then she reminds me of a tired housewife who has slipped away to the beauty parlor, comfortable in her faded work dress and run over slippers, her head stuck in a hair dryer, dreaming away the winter afternoon. Yet when the winds are just right, her tops are blown clear, leaving her lower slopes shrouded in mystery. Then she is a young girl on her way to the dance with a shawl of the most exquisite fabric draped across her lovely shoulders.

Her most ethereal mood she saves for just a very few mornings in deepest winter. When a pre-dawn fog forms and then the temperature drops, the mists freeze on the highest levels.

As the slanting rays of the morning sun touch her, each tree, limb, and twig seem to be dipped in liquid silver, and she is a fairy lady of the most delicate etchings. And yet, as I delight in the magic scene, I often cannot suppress a chuckle, for in all her fragile loveliness she presents a most comical illusion. I see in her the specter of an old maid aunt, doing the weekly baking, slightly tipsy from sampling the cooking sherry. She has somehow managed to spill the flour, and a gentle cloud of white has settled over her head and shoulders. She goes about her work, unaware of her appearance, still presenting a prim and proper face to her family. And they, respecting her position, pretend nothing is amiss.

For many years I have observed this old mountain, watching as she slowly changed her costumes to fit each season. I have long admired her beautiful lines, the softness of distant trees following her contours, the hint of rock and cliff glimpsed through the foliage. But now, that lovely picture has changed! The change has been gradual. At first I didn't notice. Then, as the changes progressed, I became accustomed to them, and could no longer see the effect. But now, taking a new look through fresh eyes, I finally can recognize what has happened, and shudder at the results.

Where before I saw only trees, now I also see driveways and patios. Instead of deer paths, I see roads. Her lovely lines are marred by the squares, cubes and sharp angles of houses. Her appearance is blotchy, the dissonant whites, grays and browns of man's creations clashing with her natural shadings. It's almost as if she has developed some sort of a rash that has slowly but steadily climbed her slopes, reaching ever higher. Where will it end?

Progress has come to my old friend. I suppose such progress is good: good for the county and good for the economy in general. It's probably even good for those who have such a surplus of funds that they can afford to spend ridiculous sums to build on a steep mountain slope so they can enjoy the magnificent view.

I do not begrudge them their dream castles, if such they be. But did they have to rape my old friend for their pleasure?

My October Days

by Alma Stiles Bryson

October's blue sky is vivid azure
With billowing clouds climbing ever higher
Like whipping cream creeping
Over the top of a bowl.
Jets draw white tic-tac-toe games
Across the vast expanse of blue sky.
Cool morning fog creeps like a giant
Albino leopard into each valley,
Twitching his long tail into the road
Blocking my view as I drive to school.
Warm afternoons crickets build
Their chorus to a crescendo.
Butterflies sip at mud puddles,
Flitting about quickly. Do they know
The time is short, that winter approaches?
Apple trees sag with the weight of harvest.
Grapes smell mouth-watering good.
They're ready for gathering.
Cane is stripped of blades of green then
Pressed for juice for sorghum molasses.
The sweet aroma hitches a ride on
Every current of air. Silage is ground
Of corn. The fragrant green stalks blend
The sweetness in open pits to ferment.
That becomes winter feed for cattle.
Dogwood berries change to scarlet,
Decorating as if for a celebration.
Leaves change colors and fall in the
Many breezes, making a spectacle of
Themselves. Then the cool rain, always
Cooler gently falls causing leaves to ripple
Like a tiny army is marching on them.
From my classroom I hear playgrounds
Vibrate. Yellow buses collect their squealing
Cargo to go home. Then all is quiet.

The Wreath-Ribbon Quilt

by Ruth Moose

We sit waiting for Christmas, strangers whose lives are linked by blood, marriage, and memories. This is a rare calm. From the living room my daughters' voices float in a kind of music as they giggle and talk, shake packages and bells.

My brother, Gary, tall in his blue V-neck sweater, flips channels on television, a montage of people, snow scenes, disasters, and commercials on digestion aids. The first year Gary went off to college it seemed he grew like a hollyhock. At his wedding I noticed for the first time he was taller than Daddy. Gary's wife, Anne, sits in the Boston rocker and feeds their six-month-old baby. Bubbles in her bottle float to the top, work like yeast.

Beside me on the sofa, Henry, my husband, leafs through an ancient issue of *Reader's Digest*. The corners are so curled he must press them flat to read, "I am Joe's Heart."

This lull is strange. Not peaceful, for there is a touch of tension present, but for the first time in days, I begin to relax. No cookies to roll, cut, and sugar-sprinkle, no gifts to wrap, ribbons to fluff and tie; my hands, not in motion, lie like clay birds in a nest behind my knees.

My father's chair is empty. A blue plastic recliner, it looms large, casts a square shadow in the corner.

Mother bangs a spoon in the kitchen stirring oyster stew. We always have oyster stew on Christmas Eve, but before, Daddy in a red striped apron, arms at angles like airplane wings, tasted and stirred. He heated it slowly, peppered, paprikaed twice, made us wait until he pronounced the thick broth creamy-perfect.

Gary, on the sofa now, moves an embroidered pillow, sits beside Henry. They discuss the Super Bowl, who's to win. Their talk turns to cars and Gary moans the loss of the sweet sports car he traded for Anne's station wagon.

"I could feel it," Anne says quickly. "He used to scare me half to death. Could have killed us both trying to see how much that car would do. I told him to either drive with sense or let me out. God, he tried to fly the thing."

My legs prickle under me and the sofa becomes a lush automobile seat. Daddy makes the speedometer needle move from 80 to 90 and past. My mother screams, "What are you trying to do? Kill us all?

Make the car fly? Stop and let me out. You can kill yourself if you want to, but let me and the baby out." I watched the needle ease slowly back; the trees become trees out of the green fuzzy blur. The wind noise stops and my father, not laughing any longer, is angry, his face red as strawberry cake. Mother lets her breath out slowly and loud. My legs relax against the seat.

Mother comes from the kitchen, wipes her hands on her white apron, and pushes a footstool near Anne and the baby. She pats the baby's pink-knitted-bootie feet. "I'm surprised she can still wear these. She's growing so fast."

The baby smiles. Milk trickles from the corner of her mouth and down her hill of a chin. "If you don't want the rest of this–"Anne holds the bottle up. The baby reaches out a starfish hand, settles quickly back.

"I haven't made oyster stew in so long." Mother pushes back her hair. "I didn't know if I would remember how...and the only oysters I could find seemed small."

I used to fish oysters, large as shells, lift them from my bowl to Daddy's. He'd make some joke about lead in his pencil.

My daughters run in from the living room and swing onto Henry's lap. Jackie hugs his neck, whispers loudly toward his ear, "Can't we open just *one* present now?"

Henry glances at me. "No, let's wait. It won't be much longer." He tickles her stomach and she folds up laughing. Kate joins them in the horseplay.

I remember Daddy teasing me, making me wait, the suspense and surprise a mixture of aching delight. Now Christmas seems a whirlwind of duties, demands. Even the gifts we give and get are practical: pajamas and robes, toaster-ovens and fry pans. Last year I gave Gary, as a joke, a book, *Making Wine at Home*. Anne told me later the only thing they got was a jug of the darkest vinegar and a stain the size of a dinner plate on their kitchen ceiling.

Daddy used to make wine. I wonder if Gary remembers. Daddy made it before there were books on the subject, before wine-making was a fad kind of thing to do. He had wooden kegs in the basement and the air smelled purple, later a fuzzy gray. His wine, like Gary's, failed. He rolled kegs onto the grass, removed the plugs, let dark liquid, the color of blood, gush over on the green lawn. Mother came out to ask if it would hurt the grass. Daddy didn't answer.

One of the girls, Jackie, whines at Henry's elbow, "I don't see why we can't open one present now."

Henry says after we eat they can open all the presents. Mother says if they don't stop fussing, Santa Claus will hear them and not bring the Teresa Tresses dolls they want.

They never saw my father as Santa Claus. The suit he rented sagged and bunched under the wide, black plastic belt. His curled beard could have covered two chins. After a drink or two at each of the first dozen homes Daddy visited, stomping snow from his boots and ho-hoing louder as the night moved on, he would have to hire someone to drive the car. Gary refused. He said if Daddy wanted to make a fool of himself at his age, he didn't want to be present to see it. When someone brought Daddy home, heavy after midnight, he was dressed in regular clothes. I never knew what happened to the Santa Claus suit.

Mother goes to the closet, rumbles in it. "You can't wait, can you, honey?" She gives the girls a box of toys. There is a rusty wind-up drummer boy Gary used to have. It lies broken on top. Hanging from one corner is a doll I never liked. She is wigless and her scalp a patch of sticky lint.

Kate carries the box to the living room. Mother winks at me. "That should keep them busy a little while. Their minds off opening presents, at least until the stew gets ready."

She pulls a plastic bag from a closet shelf, takes out a rainbow of ribbons. "Do you want these?" She strokes the ribbons, pulls a green one through her fingers.

"What?" I can't think why I would want the ribbons. They are too large for the girls to wear, if they ever wore such things, too limp for bows, too wide for gift wrapping. "Where did you get them?"

"Your father's funeral." She looks surprised that I had to ask. "The wreaths. I took them off the wreaths." She lays ribbons in a row down her arm. "They've been washed and pressed."

My head aches from the smell of carnations. A room filled and hot with carnations.

"You can make a coverlet," Mother says. "I've seen some beautiful ones. All ribbons of the same colors can be a border, others worked into a pattern."

I see Mother pluck bows from each wreath, gathering her arms full like a garden bouquet. "No." I shake my head. "No."

She's disappointed. I think of the hours she's spent unwinding wires, washing ribbons, the work to iron satin without scorching.

"There's enough purple ones," she holds several ribbons the color of awards. "They'd make a nice border."

"You keep them. You make a coverlet." I look to Henry for help He's hiding in his reading. The *Reader's Digest* is desperation. I wish he'd notice what's happening, change the subject, say something, say anything.

Gary holds the baby, Lucinda. He pats her back until she burps loudly. "Atta girl," he says and kisses the top of her head wobbling on its stem of neck.

Anne restacks the diaper bag, folds in a terrycloth bib.

"I thought you'd want them." Mother closes the bag, stuffs it back into the closet. Her dress is a Christmas red. She never wore black or navy blue, not even to the funeral.

Ribbons the color of carnations. In my mind I see the wreaths still, my father's frozen face, the scar untouched; not even the undertakers would try to camouflage it. The scar that was a ditch of cuts and bruises, his face a mass of purple and red that night. "Go, you old tomcat, you," my mother screamed at him. He stood, head on his arms resting against the wall like someone being searched. "You got what you deserved," she yelled. "Some woman's husband came home too soon."

Gary, eyes bright with fever, dark hair limp, sat on her lap, hand over his ear. An infection woke him screaming in the night. Mother had been rocking, I heard him cry, the even *whump, whump* of the rocker, was almost asleep again when Daddy came home and the argument began. Mostly an argument in Mother's voice. I stumbled sleepily into a room of people I knew but did not know. Mother pointed at Daddy, then the door. "Go on," she said. "Don't make me look at the mess you are."

He said something, pried my hands loose, and left. I didn't run after him and for the rest of the night, and several after, kept hearing his returning footsteps that weren't there.

In the weeks he was gone, Mother never used his name. I don't know what she told the neighbors, her friends, Mr. Edwards at the lumber company. If he was missed by anyone but me, if she was worried he wouldn't come back, I didn't know.

He did come back, one night. I came in for breakfast and he was in his place at the table buttering toast, his face healed except for the scar. He didn't look at me and I strangled on my orange juice. Mother came to lift my arm, help me stop coughing, but I ran to the bathroom. Daddy was gone when I got back. "Where's Daddy?"

"Gone to work," she said, and started clearing the table. Daily routines became routine again, no questions were asked, at least not in my presence, nor explanations given. The scar across Daddy's face stayed dark and ragged the rest of his life.

Mother startles me by slamming the closet door, saying, "I better check the stew. It may be boiling over. Goodness." Then she calls me to set the table.

I arrange crackers in a basket. She says it would be nice if we had some sprigs of artificial pine or holly to tuck in for color.

Jackie, my five-year-old, runs in, holds out a toy. "Look." The toy is a plastic skull the size of a shrunken head.

"Where did you get this?"

"The toy box."

Mother ladles stew. "That thing." She hands me a bowl to put on the table. "I found it in the yard raking leaves. Some child dropped it Halloween."

"It's horrible. Ugly."

"Let's see if it still works." Mother presses a tear-shaped spot on the skull's forehead. Its eyes light red, blink; a harsh, grinding sound begins.

Jackie holds the skull to her ear like a shell. "It's laughing."

The tinnish laughter gets louder, grates on.

My father laughed at death when he watched the speedometer needle rise, when he talked of minefields, buddies blown up in his lap. Nobody dies until their time comes, he said. I worried for years he'd crash in a car, get a shotgun blast in the chest, or be found bloody in somebody else's bed. He died in his chair, newspaper spread across his knees. His reading glasses fell to the floor, dropped but did not crack.

I snatch the screaming skull and throw it like a grenade out the kitchen door.

"Don't let cold air in." Mother puts another bowl of stew on the table. "Let's eat while this is hot."

Lucinda starts to fuss when Anne puts her in the infant seat. She wiggles and waves her arms until I pick her up.

"Go ahead and eat," I tell everyone. "We'll go see the tree."

"Lights," I tell Lucinda. She finds my face more interesting. Eyes that blink and are wet. With a warm finger, she traces silver trickles down my cheeks, laughs. I am holding her tighter than I realize. She squirms to be free.

Silent Eulogy

by Paul Donovan

There we were at the graveyard's chapel, my hand on his casket. I knew all eyes were on me when the priest asked, "Is there anything anyone wishes to say?" I, of course, was the most logical person in the room to give a eulogy. After all, I was somewhat of a man of words; I had written and marketed many of my poems over the years. I was the oldest son. My mother often said, "You always did have the gift of Blarney."

I said nothing. I touched his casket one more time, wiped the tears from my eyes and said, "Good-bye Dad." I walked away in silence. After all, what could I say? I didn't know him. I knew him to be a kind, gentle, loving man, but I never really knew his innermost emotions; the war buried those.

I was four years old when he came home from World War II. My grandmother was primarily responsible for those first four years of my life. My mother worked for *the cause*, at a company named Mine Safety. I never did ask what she did, and it was many years later before I would understand what *the cause* was.

I can hardly remember my own name anymore, but I clearly recall that day fifty-two years ago. I was upstairs in my room at my grandparents' home when my mother called to me.

"Come down and see who's here." I walked down three steps and stopped dead in my tracks. They were all there at the bottom of the stairway with huge smiles on their faces. Descending the stairway, looking over the banister, was a hallway that led to the kitchen. They were lined up like ducks in a row with my grandfather closest to the kitchen, my grandmother next to him. At the bottom of the stairway my mother stood, and finally, a tall, skinny dude in a soldier's uniform.

Everyone was beaming at me as if I had accomplished a great feat. I didn't bother to smile back. When you're four years old you can't trust four grinning adults. You know they're up to something and in my family, you know it could have been almost anything. My mother moved the scenario on by asking me if I knew who that tall, skinny dude was. "Uncle Chick?" I answered.

"No," she said.

"Uncle Denny?"

"No."

To make a long story short, I went through all five of my mother's brothers and probably would have gone on to the neighbors if she hadn't stopped me cold with, "Paul, this is your father."

It was the only time in my life that I slid down the banister and didn't get in trouble. I couldn't get there fast enough. I jumped into his arms knocking his peaked hat off to the side, pushed myself back from him and asked, "Are you really my dad?"

He said simply, "Yes, Son, I am."

I guess I fell into a state of ecstasy because I don't remember much more of that day except for all the people coming and going and me telling everyone "This is my dad!"

I do remember when my day came to a close, and he carried me up the stairs and tucked me into bed for the very first time. He sat on the side of the bed with mom standing behind him. He pulled me close to him and whispered, "I'm home, Son, for good."

I'm told, I responded, "Well it's about time!" As they were leaving the room, and he was closing the door behind him, I yelled "I'm glad you're home, Daddy!"

He whispered, "So am I Son, so am I."

We lived with my mother's parents for awhile longer as my dad looked for work. As it turned out, his father had been working for the electric company and was able to help get him an entry level position there. The only problem was it became necessary to move so he could be closer to work. I, for one, was not overly enthused with that idea.

My father never had a car in his entire life. It was rumored that he was in an accident as a teenager, and there were some friends killed, others badly injured. It was never discussed, just as none of his childhood was ever divulged. The only thing I knew, was that my parents were married while my father was an usher in a movie theater, and he was making only eleven dollars a week. My brother and I became privy to this information whenever it was felt we needed, the *value of money* sermon.

Not having his own transportation forced my father to rely on co-workers who were close by to drive him to work for a nominal fee. When there was no one nearby working the same shift, he was placed in the position of having to take several connecting buses and walk over the Island Bridge in every kind of imaginable weather.

I don't recall ever hearing him complain. It was understandable that when he did spend some time at home, he'd fall asleep in his favorite chair until it was time to go to bed. I recall one time when he did this. I tied his arms to the chair, lit a piece of paper under his nose, and yelled, "Fire!"

He tried to jump up, screamed, "What the hell!" When he realized what had happened, he sat back in his chair and had a good hearty laugh, for which I was thankful. He wasn't devoid of humor then, just too tired to enjoy it. These were primarily the reasons why he wasn't there for me at ball games, school functions, and other all-around growing up situations. We never did catch up with each other.

I'll Be Home for Christmas

by Jerry R. Houser

That short phrase, no doubt, carries many different connotations to different folks throughout our fair land. To me, those words have always held a special significance due to my mother's lifelong love of that holiday season. This feeling was transmitted to my brother, sister and myself in our earliest memories. Like her mother, Mama Sue, my mother was a music teacher. It was her lot in life to end up in a small west Texas town with three infant children whose father had departed for Alaska in search of streams full of gold or, Lord only knows, what other rainbows might strike his fancy.

The time was the early 1930's, the Great Depression was in full bloom, and she had no resources available to her other than her education at the Chicago Music Conservatory and her determination. So armed, she hung out her sign proclaiming Piano–Voice Lessons and started building a following of equally determined mothers. Possibly, like other children of that era, I have always thought that the old saying, *We'll make do*, was spawned by our elders during those difficult times.

But in the eyes of young children, they were wonderful times, particularly during the Christmas season. In early December the dog-eared storybooks would resurface, and the attention of siblings and myself would shift from mumbley-peg and doodlebugs to reindeer and visions of sugarplums. But as we aged and more fully understood the mechanics of Santa's arrival, we came to a startling realization. We had no fireplace in the house, no hearth and, most importantly, no chimney. Ed, my older brother, brought this dilemma to the attention of my sister Susie and me. That led to the disturbing conclusion. No chimney, no Santa.

Faced with three teary-eyed kids, my mother had to make the difficult choice of dispelling the myth of Santa or accommodating it. So she and my uncle built a hearth in the living room. Family pictures show us expectantly sitting before it on the floor. We believed, we truly believed that sometime during that magical Christmas Eve night Santa would come out of that hearth. Never mind that it contained a gas stove rather than embers or that the chimney was not actually visible, we believed because Mom, as ever, had *made do*. Each year, about two weeks prior to the big day, we would don our warmest clothes, climb into the old Hudson auto and head for the hills to seek our annual tree. But, in west Texas, there are no pines nor spruce nor virtually any other type of tree except scrub cedar. And to compound the problem, the winds that roared across the plains would bend and twist the limbs unmercifully until they were woefully misshapen.

Thus we would scour the barren landscape for trees that had different components: a good top and trunk here; nice middle limbs there; then boughs for the hearth. When Mom made the judgment that we had all the necessary pieces, we would commence loading limbs, branches and trunks on top and in the rear of the car. As we moved down the highway, I'm sure we were mistaken for a moving nursery more than once.

Arriving home, all was moved into the living room and the assembly would begin. Aided by a nail here, piano wire there and a ball of twine, we shifted and adjusted each limb under Mom's direction and to the accompaniment of carols on the record player. Then, standing at a distance, my mother would always declare it *perfect, the best one ever,* which was our signal to start decorating our creation.

Over the years, Mom's teaching practice flourished, we grew, the world went to war, and all things in our lives seemed to change. All except our Christmas traditions. From gathering around the piano as youngsters to sing carols with Mom and neighbors, we expanded our invitation list until Christmas Eve would see fifty to sixty folks pass through our doors to visit, sing and enjoy pastries and punch. It was truly the most wonderful time of the year. Understandably, Mom's feeling for the season passed to us three kids, and we always made every effort to be home for Christmas.

After graduating from college I entered the Air Force and subsequently to pilot and gunnery training. Ultimately I was assigned to the Far East. It was during that time that I missed my first Christmas at home. Rather than the wind-swept plains of west Texas, I saw the jungles of the Philippines, the islands of Okinawa and Formosa and the countryside of Japan. Christmas Eve circa 1954 found me huddled under a pile of rice and straw-filled comforters in a Japanese hostel. I vowed that, come what may, I would be home the next year.

And what came in the next year was considerable. In fact, it was a tumultuous year in which our fighter squadron was jerked from a rather idyllic existence in the Philippines to the less balmy climes of Okinawa and Formosa. The Korean truce was tenuous at best as confrontations along the demarcation line became more frequent and bloody. The

Chinese Communists continued their own private war with the Chinese Nationalists who had retreated from the mainland to Formosa. The Chi-com turned up the heat by laying territorial rights to Quemoy and Matsu and laid siege to the two insignificant little islands.

The U.S. backed Chi-nats retaliated with daily bombing runs to the mainland and things appeared to be going to hell in a hand-basket as the Chi-coms massed fighter squadrons and army divisions along their coastline and made clear their avowed intention to add Formosa to their real estate holdings. Chinese necks and U.S. prestige were on the line when the U.S.7th Fleet sailed into the straits separating the combatants and drew the line down the middle of those frigid waters.

The result was that the fleet steamed back and forth while the Navy fighters flew low cover, the Air Force fighters flew mid-cover and the Chi-com MIG's flew top-cover above us all. A scenario that made all of us good-guy pilots a little nervous to say the least. The saber-rattling continued until negotiators cut a deal that allowed evacuation of the two disputed islands and other concessions. The fragile peace was maintained for the moment, and all the players went back from whence they had come. Little did we know that the introduction of U.S. advisors into Vietnam was only five years away.

But the year had taken its toll. I had lost three squadron compatriots to mid-air collisions and one to a low-altitude bailout from his flaming Sabre-jet. Tired of the dismal weather of Formosa and Okinawa, I was ready to go home. My tour coming to an end, my request for leave enroute to my next duty station in Arizona was granted. The trip to the other side of the world was arduous, and after two days of non-stop travel I arrived in Dallas, Texas and decided to finish the trip by train. For the moment, I didn't want to see another transport plane. Boarding the early morning Texas-Pacific, I slumped into a window seat and was asleep in moments.

Hours later, I awoke to the smell of coffee and sway of the train. The seats opposite mine were vacant except for the one on the aisle. There sat a wizened little man who accepted a cup of coffee from the porter with a whispered and repeated, "I 'preciate it."

Receiving my cup of brew, I raised it toward the man in salutation. He nodded barely then resumed blowing on the cup and sipping it alternately. He wore a Stetson hat with a curled brim, and his suit had a western cut, neat but slightly shiny. The white shirt was frayed around the collar and topped by a bandanna-style kerchief strung through a shiny silver cow's head. The latter two appeared to be rather new, and

I surmised that they were worn only to funerals and weddings. His boots bore signs of fresh polish, but both heels and soles were worn on the outside. No doubt he walked the way he rode, bowlegged. As I studied him, his gray-blue eyes glanced at me momentarily then back straight ahead. Long furrows creased his tan weathered face, and his gnarled hands had obviously grasped many a saddle-horn and strand of barbed wire. He was short and compact, and I imagined that he had probably broken a few mustangs in his time. Having been raised in his country, I gauged his age could range from forty to sixty-five. There was a disturbing aura of sadness about him.

This time, when he glanced my way our eyes locked, and I realized that I was staring at him. Embarrassed, I mumbled something like, nice tie, to which he nodded and said "I 'preciate it", twice. There was a momentary silence.

He leaned closer and stated matter-of-factly, "You're a military, aren't you?"

A bit puzzled by the expression, I explained that I was in the Air Force and said, "Yes I am a military." Another silence prevailed as he now studied me from head to toe. I guess I passed muster since he moved to the chair directly across from mine.

"My boy, Jimmy Joe, actually my little girl's boy, is a military. His daddy was an oil-field man and took off. Then she took off looking for him and neither of them ever come back. So I raised him—me and Loddy-B did. She's the colored lady down the road. We raised him 'till he joined the military. He liked it a lot, and I guess they liked him because they made him a...a... what you call it...sergeant?" I could only nod as he continued.

"Then they sent him to Ko-rea. He didn't like that place but said they needed him there, so it was okay. He wrote me and Loddy-B a lot. He was a good boy. A hard worker...helped me string a lot of wire."

The little man lapsed into meditation for a moment, and I asked where he was headed. "We're going home to Cohoma. I've got a little spread out there." He nodded toward the window at the vast prairie lands dotted by scrub cedar, tumbleweed and cactus. "When I heard he was coming home, I figured the least I could do was meet him in Dallas, so I did."

A bit perplexed by his remark, I looked around the coach but saw no one in uniform. I asked hesitantly, "Well, where is he now? I'd like to meet him."

The man appeared pained by the question. His lip twitched as he spoke almost inaudibly, and with a jerk of his thumb, "He's back there–in the baggage car, in a box…a casket." Another twitch, then, "They said he got killed in Ko-rea. Said he was protecting some spot, some line. Them Ko-reans shot him."

Stunned by his statement, I could only offer my regrets to which he nodded his head and muttered, "I 'preciate it". Then, "and I know he'd 'preciate it too, you both being military, you know."

We sat in silence, both staring out the window until on the outskirts of Big Spring. Then, he cleared his throat, and spoke, "You're an officer, aren't you?"

"Yes sir, a First Lieutenant," I replied.

"I thought so. He sent me a picture of him and his officer. Had the same kind of bars as is on you. Guess he was a Lieutenant. They shot him too–them Ko-reans did."

Then I recalled an article I'd read in the Stars and Stripes while still on Formosa. It stated that an officer and enlisted man were killed while on night patrol. Evidently their jeep had wandered into no-man's land across the demarcation line. It had to have been the same occurrence.

Ashamed that I had not done so before, I extended my hand to introduce myself. His grip was like steel as he shook once and withdrew his hand, saying, "Roy Jones is mine."

Then he startled me when he asked, "Mr. Lieutenant, do you think you could come to my boy's burying. I'd hate to have him put in the ground with only me and Loddy-B there. I mean, he went to school on the bus and such kind, but I never knew if he had any friends, us living on the spread and him working with me all the time. I don't know nothing about these kinds of things 'cause the only person I ever buried was my wife, and it was just me and her then. They's only one burying ground in Cohoma, and they said they're going to do it at two o'clock tomorrow afternoon. I know he'd 'preciate you being there, I mean you both being military, you know."

As the train pulled before the station, I stammered as I tried to respond. I explained that I needed to spend time with my family, that my mother had an annual Christmas Eve party and that I had shopping to do. When I ran out of excuses, he said simply, "I understand Mr. Lieutenant, but if you could, we'd sure 'preciate it, me and him." With that we shook hands again and parted.

My mother and our dear family friend, Carmena, were waiting at the train door as I stepped out, and I was home. After much hugging and shouting, we walked to the station to await my duffel bag. Standing in front, I watched as a group of funeral home attendants loaded the casket into a hearse. As Mr. Jones opened the car door on the passenger side, he turned and our eyes again met. He raised his right hand just slightly in a sign of recognition, and then entered the hearse which pulled away.

"Who was that man?" my mother asked. When I related the circumstances of our meeting and his final request of me, Mother and Carmena asked simultaneously, "Well, are you going?"

"I don't know. There's so much I have to do and..."

Their disdainful looks stopped me short. "Well, I'll see what I can do," I said, and we dropped the subject.

The next day, on my early morning walk, I again marveled at the contradictions of west Texas weather. This day the sky was cobalt blue, the horizon was limitless and the air crisp. How well I knew that a blowing norther could cross the plains, with little notice, carrying with it a cloud of red sand that would obliterate all in its path and drop temperatures thirty degrees within an hour. But the morning was beautiful, and the prospect for a wonderful day and Christmas Eve reunion with our many friends was exhilarating. The morning was filled with many phone calls, visits and errands, but as noon approached, my thoughts kept turning to the little man as he climbed into the hearse.

As I walked into the house, my mother looked at her watch but spoke not a word.

"I'm going! I'm going!" I said.

Smiling smugly she said, "Your uniform is in the closet. I took it to the cleaners between piano lessons and Harry cleaned it while I waited."

"Reads me like a book," I thought, as I pinned on wings, bars and my lone campaign ribbon. I blew her a kiss as I headed for her car and Cohoma. A quick stop at the local gas station secured me directions to the cemetery located on the edge of town. I raced down a dusty dirt road fearful of being late for the service. Over a slight knoll I could see an archway with a cross centered on it. Swinging around a bend, I was surprised by the large number of cars and sizeable congregation inside the picket fence that was half covered with blown sand. Parking and stepping out, I slipped on my hat, straightened my coat and walked to the back of the group still not knowing if I was at the right funeral. Then I saw Mr. Jones sitting under the canopy with a frail Negro lady with graying hair seated beside him, head bowed. Slowly, he raised his head and scanned the crowd around him. As our eyes met, he raised his hand in the same gesture as before, and I saw him smile for the first time—very faintly, but a smile.

When the minister concluded his prayer, the multitude of heads rose as the Army Honor Guard stepped forward and fired the customary salvos. As the soulful call of taps concluded, the color guard removed and folded the flag draped over the coffin and handed it to the Sergeant-in-Command. Hesitating a moment, he looked around the group then marched sharply around them and before me.

He snapped a salute which I perplexedly returned as he spoke, "Lieutenant, sir, Mr. Jones requested that, if you arrived, you make the presentation of the flag to the lady beside him."

With a lump in my throat, but in proper military manner, I marched with the sergeant to stand before Loddy-B. I presented the flag to the sobbing gray-haired lady with tears running down her face. Then Mr. Jones and I shook hands in his unusual fashion. Leaning down, I said, "Appears you and your boy had a few more friends than you imagined?"

With that faint little smile on his face, he responded, "Does appear so, doesn't it Mr. Lieutenant?"

Back home that evening, I stepped outside to get a picture through Mom's picture window. Framed by the window were my mother playing one piano, my sister playing the other and my brother and a passel of friends grouped around in song.

Shades of Norman Rockwell, it was truly wonderful to be Home For Christmas. My appreciation of the moment was greatly heightened when I thought of Mr. Jones and his boy.

Then I stepped inside to the warmth of home, hearth and friends.

Winter

by Dorothea S. Spiegel

When wintertime comes to the mountains
bare branches make windows that show
an expanded world, with vistas
        not seen by October people,

who come for the colorful autumn
and go before the leaves fall.
I see mountains tipped with tree-frost,
        and a church; I see its steeple.

Now the sun can reach my house; it's
shining through my kitchen window.
There's a spring behind that rock, there,
        sending water down to the creek.

There's a house just built last summer;
there's another on that mountain
where I saw the bear last winter.
        There are squirrels playing hide and seek.

I'm so glad I stay through winter
in these mountains that I love.
Even when the days are cloudy
        I can always look outside

and watch the birds come to the feeder.
On a clear, cold day there's sunshine
making speckles on the tree-frost.
        Bright views to see; I'll take a ride.

Musings on Love, Rain, a Few Poems, and Adolescence

by Dawn Gilchrist-Young

My tenth grade students have just finished James Joyce's *Eveline*, a short story about a young girl who chooses to keep a promise to her dying mother and live with a familiar misery, an abusive father from whom there is no protection, rather than break the promise and run away with a man she loves. As I begin this article, they begin their essays about this Eveline, this timid Joycean version of the female doormat. Most of them think she is an idiot because they are just learning of the intoxications of love in their own lives, and this makes her choice seem to them almost unimaginable. While we write it is raining outside, and I, like they, am thinking about lost loves, found loves, what keeps us safe in love, and how writers have depicted love in general.

Anytime it rains hard, like it is today, I think about the man I love. Flood warnings make him happy. Rain has always made me happy, but after marrying a man who thrives on kayaking mountain creeks nearing flood stage, I have learned yet another reason to find joy in rain. I love "love," he loves paddling, and we both love books and rain. An older and wiser friend once told me that those things alone were a sound basis for a marriage. Perhaps so. They have stood us in good stead thus far.

Poets and sages have always known that rain, among all types of weather, brings with it memories of love. Edna St. Vincent Millay wrote much about love and rain. I think about the first line from one of her sonnets, "That August should be leveled by a rain," a poem about a lost love, or the following lines:

What lips my lips have kissed, and where, and why,
I have forgotten, and what arms have lain
Under my head till morning; but the rain
Is full of ghosts tonight, that tap and sigh
From the glass and listen for reply,
And in my heart there stirs a quiet pain
For unremembered lads that not again
Will turn to me at midnight with a cry.

And there's more love, and more pain, and even more rain, but it doesn't fit here. And then, because I need cheering whenever I read or think of Millay, I recall instead the less mournful line of Robert Frost's from *A Line- Storm Song*—"Come over the hills, and far with me/ And be my love in the rain," and I think, well, that isn't too bad for a crusty, reserved New Englander who indulged in the occasional rant and petty jealousy.

Maybe there is something in the incessant and luxurious abandon of great quantities of water falling from the sky that is similar to the incessant and luxurious abandon of obsessing over a lover, especially when that someone is lost to us. Certainly, many poets have used rain as a parallel, if not a metaphor, for tears. Pablo Neruda, my pick for love poet of the ages, (even before I saw *Il Postino*, thank you), wrote, "...farewell, the tears of Nature fall." But lost loves will haunt us as long as humans have emotions. Willie Nelson, a poet of a different stripe, said in a radio interview, "Ninety-nine percent of us aren't with our first choice. That's what keeps the jukebox playing."

We think lingeringly over lost loves because they have altered our life's plan, and so we are left with the wisps of longing for what might have been, especially when we feel our own great merit goes unappreciated, perhaps, by the one who does not leave us. One way that the poet Dorianne Laux, less famous but equally wise, looks at this situation is to accept the fact that her husband, even (or maybe especially) when lying in bed beside her, thinks of women lost to him. In her mind, she says she becomes them all.

I do not know if this kind of acceptance and wisdom borne of experience, or philosophizing borne of reading, can make the preoccupation any less, but at least it allows a common perspective in the context of the universal. And at this moment, our universe still filled with rain, I wonder if the thoughts of my students are maybe filled with love, or maybe just the cramp in their writing hand. But I want them to at least know what is out there in terms of what has been written about love, and that it might help keep them safe, if only in their own heads.

I think about the German poet, Rainer Maria Rilke, how he describes Eurydice, the love lost to the mythical Orpheus, when Rilke says, "She was already loosened like long hair, and given over like fallen rain. " Perhaps that is what the adolescents I teach would like, to find someone to whom they can be "given over like fallen rain." (For that matter, perhaps that is what we all would like, although with adults, the "to whom" too often becomes the "to which" of cars, ambitions, and credit card debts.) But they, my romantic and idealistic students, still without credit card debt, write about what they see as the foolishness of Eveline, a nineteen-year-old who informs them of the mistake of giving up love for a promise made to an unreasonable parent.

They have watched the mistakes of their parents, teachers and national leaders, and from these mistakes they have understood the ultimate and inherent desirability and danger of love. They understand a great deal, and, like most adolescents of every generation enabled to articulate its woes, are themselves largely misunderstood.

They are the generation whose parents chose, for the most part, career and material goods over children, for good or ill. Their parents, (and I am included among them), are a group so dedicated to giving themselves over to the "which" that they have been little aware their children were growing up and away in the company of strangers, their toddlerhoods spent in daycare cribs and play yards, their childhoods spent in classrooms with pencils and paper, and then afterschool programs with paste, crayons, and whiffle ball. And now they are with me in this last year of their childhood, the year in which everything changes irreversibly, the seminal year of the driver's license, the newest chapter and, for them, the most real kind of freedom. After this, if they have not done so already, they will take their place in what poet Robert Lowell described as "a servile economy" that "slides by on grease." But for now they sit in yet another classroom with a hopeful, sometimes melancholy, sometimes silly English teacher who asks them to write about love on the rainiest day of this winter.

I circulate through the room, and I see they like the word *lover*" They use it often in their essays—"She had a lover," "Eveline's lover," "She had a lover who lost her to a promise." In general, the majority of them like most anything that reminds them of sex. This may be because of their stage in life, or because they have grown up in a culture that is remarkably preoccupied with sex and youth, or because of both, but it is so, and I try to use it to my advantage in getting and holding their attention. I read once that the average adolescent male thinks of sex every nineteen seconds. I have never read how often the thought of sex occurs in the average female brain, but from my own experience as a teenager, I would guess that it is just as often. In the female version, the most obvious difference might be more time spent on hand-holding and roses. When they make the occasional bawdy comment, often apropos of nothing, I like to remind them of this thought pattern. They laugh at themselves. They know better than anyone what it is to be hormonally challenged.

Here at their desks, in an atmosphere that I have consciously tried to make welcoming with my comments, encouragements, posters of movies, and a CD player from which ribbons of sound (George Winston today, maybe Albioni or Chris Thomas King tomorrow) issue, they are safe, warm, dry, and maybe thinking fine and lofty thoughts. Or maybe not. But they are still warm and dry. Ms. Millay also wrote "Love is not all: it is not meat nor drink/ Nor slumber nor a roof against rain." I, however, am not going to be the one to tell them this. I will let the school system supply the roof, meat and drink. With my infrequent lectures, I will provide the slumber. But literature, ah, literature, it will provide the vicarious knowledge of love. All too soon, my students will provide for themselves, if they have not already done so, the hands-on experience.

Nonetheless, maybe before they do, they will have gleaned enough information about human foibles and flaws in the realm of love that they will be a little easier on themselves. Or if not, maybe they will take consolation in the universality of the experience of love and passion (after all, the Latin root, "passio" means "to suffer") as exemplified in the literature of the entire planet.

In the latter half of the last century, however, and continuing today, the way children are exposed to human sexuality at earlier and earlier ages has created difficulties that present new challenges for parents, clergy, counselors, and educators. In an informed and controversial essay on the pervasiveness of *hard* pornography, Margaret Atwood raises issues concerning what sells and who is being manipulated when it comes to the formation of the human libido. Perhaps the most frightening scenario she mentions is the one in which she speculates about what happens when little girls reared on Disney's *Snow White* and *Cinderella* do when they are being courted by little boys reared, perhaps inadvertently, on the *Playboy* channel. She doesn't provide any answers in her essay, she just raises terrible questions with her descriptions of what sells as entertainment now and who has access either through television or the Internet.

I cannot really say if asking students to think about the love and suffering of a James Joyce character on a rainy day is a more wholesome alternative than Disney's depiction of human romance, but it is more realistic. I am very aware that no action of mine can protect them, safe though they are in this room. I cannot even guarantee that they will take with them anything they learn from our reading or writing, or, if they do, whether it can possibly provide anything like solace at a time when they need it, even though all the poetry I have mentioned here has, at times, provided solace for me. All I can do is offer what I know and love—that the rainiest and darkest days bring forth something in the human psyche that is beautiful and moving, that literature, at its best, makes us more completely human, and that their own thoughts and feelings, when mulled over and clarified, are worth preserving on paper. And all I can say, as they file out of the room and into the less secure but more exciting world outside, is "Stay dry. Be safe." And then, because it makes them laugh, "Abstain. Abstain. Be celibate if you can," and finally, softer but still audible, I add, "and if you can't, use protection."

Meeting Emily Dickinson On a Winter Day

by Michael L. Wright

Lowered and yellow-eyed
the gray shadows show their
seasonal hand
in this threadbare time when the grass
crunches underfoot.

    You read
    your small words
    pared and
    inscrutable

while we walk among
the crosshatched trees with
a backdrop of hoarded light
rendered in
this "one mitered day."

    Fires burn in their
    proper places and smoke lies low
    in indifferent fluency
    in this the month of the two faced god.

A shy and noiseless
noise–the air heavy with voices
stooped–the arch is low in order
to enter the smallest word–
hung like diadems undemanding.

A Beatnik Wanders Into Appalachia

and Learns the Language of the Earth and Sky

by Thomas Rain Crowe

Climbing cold streams' wet weave of root
& rock a warm murmur breathes beneath
a pool of song where water and wilt shine
on green tendrils moist with deep moss
   and dew.

Dig the dance of vine
climbing circle of stone.

Dig the blue bloom of rose
cut to caress torrents of rotting soil.

Dig the ripe wave of evening that touches flame
& breaks blood's slow boil of mulch & rain.

Walking green trees' coppered limbs of stairs
& canopy   a thrush of whistles rises in
a swoon of sunlight when thunder claps and
color arcs in clouds' turbid mood of limber logs
   and leaves.

Dig the skiff of snow that preeks soft
near the rabbit's lair.

Dig the Big Eyed Bird in swag or hollow
of locust and locked wood.

Dig the heave of new ground and the golden comb
of honey with winter rye.

Dig the dogtick and the rowan tree.

Dig the sky!

Snowshoe Rabbits

by Dick L. Michener

It's the Year of our Lord 1956, and I'm sitting in an honors class at Triumphal High School. Situated at the eastern perimeter of a small city, tucked into the folds of ancient mountains, it's a boys' school operated by Jesuits who still consider themselves papal special forces and view their curriculum as basic training for adolescent mind, body and spirit.

Whenever we venture west into high mountains, locals brand us as city slickers. Whenever we travel east into big cities, residents mock us as country bumpkins. As sophomores in a strict and demanding parochial institution, on a gloomy Wednesday morning late in March, we're not exactly sure who we are. We're dozing as wet snow drums against our classroom windows.

We're about to conclude a first period religion class taught by the Dean of Men, who is convinced, in theological as well as emotional terms, that females are truly the root of all evil. A short and bald priest with a quivering upper lip, he regales us this morning by describing precisely how *females are sewers, physically and spiritually.* He hopes that his gross depiction will keep us from impure thoughts, not to mention impure actions. He fails to realize, either that sewers can be alluring for adolescent boys, or that, so to speak, some of us already have put on our trunks, our flippers, and our snorkels, eager to dive in and explore.

Father Dean ends his lecture with this question: "Boys, suppose you have an impure thought while you're walking down a street, and, as you cross over to the other side, a Mack truck loses its brakes and squashes you flat? What happens then?"

This is the proper answer: *Father, I'm damned for all eternity.*

This is the answer which I shout just as the bell rings, much to the delight of my previously silent classmates: "I die with such a big grin on my face, Father, that a truck may flatten it, but no undertaker can remove it".

Witty comments such as this one provide the only blemishes on my report card, in the conduct section: *He's bright, and basically he's a good boy, but he does have a smart mouth.*

Our merriment abruptly ends three minutes later, as Father Football (FF in our verbal shorthand) strides into class just ahead of the bell. He played professional football before becoming a priest, back in olden times when players wore leather helmets and there was no television. He slams his books, notes and class roster down on the podium.

Because of a snowstorm early Tuesday morning, we're seeing him for the first time since Monday morning, a day when school is dismissed early because our basketball team is state champion for the first time. After attending mandatory 8:00 a.m. Mass, we're released with an admonition to spend the remainder of our holiday in thanking our Maker, not only for this championship, but for all the wonders of His creation.

My best friends and I immediately pile into my black 1940 Roadmaster, a vehicle with a miraculous interior which can expand to haul a dozen adolescent boys in complete comfort. We lead a car caravan to Sin City, in which one theater is featuring a ground-breaking movie called *And God Created Woman*. Reaching the theater just before the first showing has begun, we soon discover that this movie is ground-breaking, simply because most of it features Brigitte Bardot laying face-down on the ground, sun-bathing in her birthday suit. She displays a wondrous backside for which we are truly thankful.

Stumbling into the lobby after watching the movie twice, we're blinking our eyes when FF emerges through another door and confronts us.

"What," he snarls, "are you boys doing in this den of iniquity?"

We step backward while mumbling incoherently.

Suddenly inspired, I step forward and look straight into FF's blazing blue pupils. "With all due respect, Father, what are you doing in this den of iniquity?"

"Following the admonition of Paul, to be in the world but not of the world. To know the good and find it, boys, you need to know the bad and avoid it." He turns away and strides outside into harsh sunlight.

As FF stomps into class this dreary Wednesday morning, he glares at Trotsky, an affluent adolescent, with a prematurely receding hairline, who knows he is God's gift to females. FF snatches from Trotsky's hands a wallet-size photo which he is proudly displaying, a class portrait of his latest love, a chubby but well-endowed freshman at the girls parochial secondary school, Magisterium Academy, situated on the western perimeter of the city. In addition to teaching English at our school, FF is also chaplain at a regional hospital and carries with him a breviary marked with snapshots from nurses of all ages. Trotsky's priorities (females and fishing) duplicate those of his father, a wholesale salesman of upscale jewelry to better stores in smaller towns. FF glances at Trotsky's photo and hands it disdainfully back to him.

"Before I became a priest, Trotsky, I threw back better ones than this." FF glances again at the snapshot. "Still do."

As FF turns around toward the blackboard, Trotsky whispers loudly to the rest of us: "FF threw them back because he didn't know what to do with them, even before he became a priest."

FF whirls around, picks up Trotsky and his desk, and shakes them up and down, back and forth. We're silently wondering which is going to spew out first, the fillings in Trotsky's teeth, or the bolts in his desk.

Without looking, FF slams Trotsky and his desk downward. One leg of the desk smacks FF's right foot and, even though he wears black combat boots, he lets go of the desk, yelps in pain, and hops up and down the aisle.

Except for one student in our classroom, all of us are struggling to restrain ourselves and praying for the strength to do so, convinced that laughing at FF will put us in imminent danger of meeting our Maker prematurely.

Only Wally laughs, and he laughs so uproariously that his stomach and his voice rise and fall in paroxysms. Wally is a frequent concern of Father Principal, who is politically correct ahead of his time. He constantly reassures parents that every student always will be treated in a kind and respectful manner. In the unlikely event that inappropriate incidents occur, he urges parents to inform him immediately. The rest of us beg our parents never to contact Father Principal, but Wally's mother visits him every Monday morning to recount the injuries and injustices dealt her only child the previous week.

Most second periods on Tuesday mornings begin with FF looking down at Wally and stating dryly: "Wally's mother saw Father Principal again yesterday morning."

Just as Wally is reaching the extremities of hilarity and seems bent on demonstrating that it is possible to bust a gut while laughing, he freezes as FF whirls back around and glares down at him. Wally believes, as we all do, that he is doomed if he remains at his desk.

With a bound, Wally escapes from his desk and runs out our classroom door, FF after him. The building door bangs open and slams shut as both of them burst outside into the snow. Wally hangs a left, cuts across the front patio, and then hangs another left, proceeding down the long side past our classroom windows, FF close behind. And so it goes.

Around and around all four sides of the building race Wally and FF, reminding us of a snowshoe rabbit pursued by a ravenous fox, both of them moving with miraculous speed and agility through drifts of wet snow. Amazed that Wally actually can run so far so quickly, we realize that FF is gradually closing the gap. We know better than to cheer Wally through now open windows, but we're visualizing ourselves as snowshoe rabbits, running alongside our endangered buddy, placing him in the center of our protective pack.

Finally, Wally collapses in a heap, face-down in the center of the biggest drift, just as FF's fingers touch the back of his shirt, both of them framed in our classroom windows. Wally cannot bear to look up. FF stops, leans over, puts his hands on his knees, and takes several deep breaths. Then, he reaches down, picks up Wally, and chuckles. Tentatively, Wally chuckles back. FF carries Wally back into our building, down the hallway and into our classroom, snow and sweat dripping off both of them, and sets Wally down at his desk.

"See what I mean, boys?" All of us are puzzled.

"Remember what I told you Monday after the movie?" All of us are wary and confused.

"We're sinners, boys." All of us wait with blank expressions.

"We're sinners because we're human beings. We have failings we need to pray about and improve upon."

He shrugs. "Wally has a problem with being a whiner."

He sighs. "I have a problem with anger. I had it before I began to play football, and I kept it after I became a priest."

He pauses. "My problem's much greater, and my sin's much graver, because I'm an adult. I know better. You boys still have a lot to learn. I'm supposed to show you the ropes."

He stares at us. "I'm going to ask Wally to forgive me. I wouldn't blame him if he ran out of this classroom into Father Principal's office."

Wally thinks a moment and then shakes his head up and down. FF does the same.

"All right then, gentlemen," FF continues, "do I have your permission to begin discussion of our latest reading assignment, *The Scarlet Letter*?"

Relieved, all of us nod in agreement and take out our paperbacks. None of us minds that wind is whistling through windows still open to the storm outside.

From this day forward, Wally never mentions any injuries or injustices to his mother.

From this day forward, all of us understand that, sometimes it can be glorious to act like a man, whenever the spirit is willing, even if the flesh always is weak.

An Emerald Cloak, Trimmed in White

by John Webb

As you pass through the gap on your way down a thousand feet into the cove, something like snow blankets the ground beneath the government's white pine plantation. A shiver runs through you; it's not yet fifty degrees and too soon since the latest—and deepest—blizzard.

But it's only a carpet of spring beauty, a delicate, pink-striped white flower, not as big as a fingernail, flush with the rays of dawn under the gloomy pine boughs. Millions of the cupped blossoms spread down either side of this branch of the creek. In a few days, they'll open into stars.

As you make your way down the branch into the fuller sun and warmer air of a grove of reddening maples, you notice the white, quarter-sized, wheel-spoked blossoms of bloodroot popping up in clusters every few feet, then the first feathers in thousands of green tri-corner hats, the buds of the white, large-flowering white trillium, even a few purple stinking willie.

Beneath the canopy of nascent tulip poplar leaves, near the old orchard in the cove, the light is a wispy, delicate green. The first shoots of solomon seal and the fiddleheads of rattlesnake fern are underfoot everywhere you step, and the other worldly American mandrake unrolls its deeply scalloped leaves over acres of level cove floor.

It's hard to spot the first lily-like blades of the ramps because they're so near the same green as the May-apple too small to dig today, while the branch lettuce on the mossy rocks in the nearby spring branch is early this year—already bolted, too milky and bitter for the best eating. In a week, maybe two, the ramps will make a soporific feast. You can't eat them in any quantity without growing wonderfully drowsy.

There's one tiny, pink blossom decorating a thin branch coming out low on the dark-iron trunk of an ancient, unnamed apple. Satisfied that they're not setting fruit too soon, for a hard freeze might come yet, you head up the old road to the bald, past the tumble-down stones of chimneys, their builders long buried in forgotten graveyards decorated only by spring.

The swarming green light of the cove gives way gradually to bare hickory and oak limbs, spots of trillium and bloodroot buds, swaths of spring beauty, subdued. But here's a pleasant surprise: The sarvus are in full bloom, balls of snowflakes on the branch tips of slender, anonymous, gray trees.

As you near the bald, they crowd in, until it's like your vision of walking through the old orchard in full flower, light upon light. You know that it's safe for your taters and peas, because the sarvus never gets fooled by a freeze.

There's a dimmer blossom just beginning to crowd in among this riot of white. It's the Carolina silver bell, orderly rows of pearly white, hemispheric bells along dark branches, hanging in profusion over the abandoned trace where it meets the state road. You'll have to look quickly—they'll likely be gone in a few days while the sarvus will continue to glow against the greening grass of the bald, dimming as the trees leaf out.

Dazzled by all this pale splendor and warmed by the delicious, dusty sun on the gravel road, you hardly notice the cold east wind that walks you home from the bald and softly sings you to sleep. You dream of white blossoms wafting down in verdant sunlight onto yellow-green orchard grass. You wake at dawn to find the mountain covered with a three-inch blanket of snow.

Lutie

by Barbara C. Arnold

She was the eighth of sixteen young'uns. Didn't get much notice. Only she was the tow head one, hair halfway between gold and pure cotton and crimped like colored folks. Glowed like an angel's. I, Billy Bob, noticed her. Lutie got them little knots on her chest and was feeling right pert. She made a weddin' quilt with wood lilies on it. I saw her at the barn dance in her sashed dress doing them dancin' figures real proud.

Snod, from the moonshine folks, up on the mountain, noticed her too. I wanted to ride her home in my truck, but Snod got there first. It probably didn't matter because she was fixin' to get away from being number eight of sixteen. As I said, she was pert. That mountain and being number one looked fine to her.

She went with Snod. He was a small feller, had a limp like he was leaning into his next step, but he had a way about him. He took her to the preacher's; I'll say that for him. Only time he went near a church.

If Lutie ever got off the mountain, I didn't see her. Heard things, though. Like in 'bout three years we heard they were hungry up there. No one had good crops the summer before. By March folks had eaten up most everything. Pokes, and cresses, the green plants comin' up by the stream, weren't very filling.

I went up there with some turnips we had left. I picked a bunch of greens along the way. It was all overgrown. I come out to their place, and there she was, hoeing in her garden. Hardly anything was up. She stood there looking kind of froze, that cloud of hair like a dandelion gone to seed in the sun, sunbonnet hanging by the strings down her back. She had two young'uns and was big with another one coming. She looked quick up the mountain. I knew there was a still up there, and Snod.

"Lutie," I says, and held out the sack of turnips and the bunch of poke salad. Lutie quick pulled her bonnet up over that hair, shading her face.

"You, Billy Bob, you go 'fore there's trouble," she hissed. "I can't take your stuff. We gettin' along fine without it."

I knew that wasn't true. Even under the shadow of her sunbonnet I could see the mottled green and yeller around her eyes. Her face was thinner than I remembered.

91

"Git!" she said looking fierce as a dandelion could. She pulled up proud and shook the hoe at me.

I went and took the stuff with me. At the edge of the clearing I looked back. She was mighty small and prideful, leaning against a pole meant for hanging a scarecrow on, her hand on her belly.

Folks who happened up there said Lutie had wild flowers and ferns planted around their cabin, and the little ones had dandelion hair and were wild as deer, except Little Snoddy, who was twice as big as his Daddy and kind of stayed put.

By and by Lutie's children left, the girls to work in factories down in the towns, and Little Snoddy as far as Bird Hollow where I saw him most every day sitting on the bench in front of the store.

The sheriff figured he'd better go up and check out that still. No one had seen Big Snod around for a long time and he wondered what was going on and how Lutie was doing without her children. The first thing he noticed was the kudzu climbing on the house and to the edge of the garden. Kudzu grew real good up in that cove. Lutie was planting wild pinks around the porch. Cans of wild seedlings were lined up on the rotting boards. She stopped digging and the sheriff said she just seemed to study on him.

"Snod's gone," she said.

"Where to?" the sheriff asked.

"That's a good question," Lutie answered. "I couldn't rightly say." That was all the sheriff could get out of her.

He told Little Snoddy he better get up there and help his maw. He being so slow, after some time passed, I thought I might could go up there and find out how things were and what happened to Big Snod. Lutie was important to me.

That pesky kudzu vine was about ready to strangle the place except where the wild flowers were planted. Lutie had kept that up real good, but I could see the kudzu was fixin' to take over if she quit hoeing for one day. There was a new scarecrow, wasn't weathered at all, hung from that post, with a big old brimmed hat down over it's face, kind of slanty.

Lutie didn't answer my call. I knew she was around, her working things on the porch just out of reach of the kudzu. I went in and into where they slept. There she was, under her lily quilt, hair like one of them angel halos, on the pillow.

"Hello, Lutie," I called.

She looked up at me out of eyes cunning and wild as a fox.

"Lutie?"

She opened her mouth and she laughed, only it was more of a cackle. Her teeth were all broken off in front. She was right crazy. I could do nothing. I ran down the mountain to get some women folk, the Doc, maybe one of her daughters from the towns where the factories were.

Her daughters had moved on to other towns. No way to reach them. Folks didn't remember Lutie, only one of so many. Doc was busy delivering babies. Little Snoddy dragged his heels about going up the mountain. He was a whimperer.

"My Daddy might come back. He whup me. That's why I left. I know he's got a gun."

I all but pushed Little Snoddy up that mountain. Yes, I went up again. Seemed like I was all Lutie had. The kudzu had taken over. It ran along the porch, all over Lutie's plants. It choked her garden. It covered the scarecrow, crept up the overalls streaked with red dirt, over the faded shirt, and I smelled something nasty under that pulled down hat.

I pushed Little Snoddy into the cabin filled with growing things saved from the kudzu and now withered in cans. I pushed him into the room where Lutie lay under the lily quilt.

She was stone dead, shriveled like one of them foreign mummies. She looked fierce and proud, her eyes wide open, pert.

"Maw!" Little Snoddy shrieked and tore out of the house like she was after him. He sat on the steps and cried.

I pulled the lily quilt decent over Lutie's face and her crinkly tow hair and went to Snoddy. We had to go down the mountain to Bird Hollow and arrange for a burial. Little Snoddy passed the garden covered with kudzu and the slanty scarecrow smothered with vine. It was so still-like, watching him. Made me cold.

Snoddy looked nervous back over his shoulder. He screamed, "It's him! It's leaning like my Daddy! It's him under there!"

Remembered Laughter

by Autumn Woodward

The old woman sits on her porch,
Watching the dawn creep slowly over the mountains.
While the mist turns the color of grape hyacinths,
And a red tailed hawk floats on the morning wind.

The cool air smells of daffodils,
And the pungent fragrance of hemlocks.
Of wet ferns and rain soaked earth,
Mingling with the soft scent of herbs.

Lavender, rosemary, mint and anise,
They are planted between the spokes of an old wagon wheel,
The wood once painted red,
Now grayed with age.

A rough-hewn wooden bench sits beneath the old cherry tree,
The broken handle of a hoe leans against it,
Waiting to be repaired and put to use in the vegetable garden,
Long hidden beneath a sea of weeds.

Bees buzz around their nest in the grape arbor,
And a cricket chirps in the wet grass.
A dragonfly hovers over the well,
Crumbling stones lost under a cascade of honeysuckle vines.

Violets spread in a sea of purple and green,
Blooming among the stones of the pathway.
They flourish here, where the footsteps no longer fall,
Like amethysts, scattered on the smooth, weathered rocks.

Over the porch, the clay chimes tinkle softly,
As if trying, somehow, to recapture the songs and laughter,
The music of the fiddle, and the notes of the banjo,
All now still.

The sun heaves itself above the ridge at last,
But the woman is gone. The hawk too
Has disappeared. Yet the creak of the rocker
Echoes through the morning stillness.

Lace Shawl

by Mary Michelle Brodine Keller

The signs says Estate Sale, code words,
someone died, usually a grandmother,
mother or elderly aunt, the men already gone.

Two great-nieces sit in overstuffed chairs
drawn to an early American table, topped
with Japanese Hummels and sandwiches
on waxed paper, potato chips and half-full cola cans.

This is part of the ritual of letting go.
After all, no one wants Aunt Mae's old things.
The great-nieces live in new vinyl houses,
decorated with designer furniture of pressed wood,
poly-acrylic protected, permanent-press pricillas,
and rent-to-own.

Put up that sign and strangers rush
in where family fears to tread.
I am one of those strangers.
I walk reverently through the house. After all,
she well could have passed in this room.
Not wanting to appear insensitive, a vulture,
I examine, measure with care the leavings,
those in sight of the great-nieces...mourners.

In the bedroom I quickly sum up a life's accumulation,
unused gifts from sons and daughters, worn quilts
pieced by her mother, polyester dresses and slips,
straps pinned shorter with safety pins. I untangle
a lace shawl tossed on the floor in a cardboard box.
Aunt Mae had run a string through the top cupping
it to fit her frail shoulders. I hold it up, admire
the flower tracings tatted into the triangle of silky fringe.
It cannot be much, an old woman's shawl.

B. J. King and the Big, Fancy Church

by Mary Lou McKillip

In my fondest memories, I recall the old grist mill and country store as they sat in the valley near Cherokee, North Carolina with the big, fancy church house on the hill.

I have seen many changes in my lifetime and many precious, old time ways lost. When I was a small lad growing up at the turn of the century, I remember the creek that ran into the Pigeon Forge river.

Dad, Mama and us young'uns lived about three miles from there in a little run-down shack we called home. It was wonderful growing up in the Smoky Mountains.   Seemed like only God, us and the birds knew how peaceful it was.

The grist mill and country store were run by their owner, Mr. B. J. King. He had a fine grist mill and store with everything your heart desired, but couldn't afford.   Mr. B. J. and his wife, Molly, had a two-story house on the hill above the store and mill. You had to cross the creek to get to his place of business and home. The old rock bridge that crossed the creek looked like pictures I have seen of England and Scotland, with flowers and cattails growing alongside the creek.

One day my dad overheard B. J. talking as how he'd been to Ohio and saw a big, white, fancy church house with colored glass windows and how he was going to build one just like it here for the folks in the mountains of Cherokee.

B. J. said if anyone would donate trees he'd have them cut and sawed into lumber for the new church house, being as how he had a saw mill on Snowbird Mountain near Robbinsville.

A town meeting was held in B. J's roomy store around the big pot-belly stove. Everyone was excited about the new church house and each said they would donate about ten to twenty trees.   There were about forty to fifty houses scattered over the hills and valleys. Everybody had trees on their land. That was about all of their wealth except for the land they owned. Most folk had a milk cow, hogs, some laying hens and horses to pull their wagons. And, back then, they had about twelve or thirteen children. They had to do something to the pass time.

B. J. offered to donate land to build the church house on. It would be about in his front yard, but folks said they didn't mind if he didn't. My mama and Molly, along with ladies of the community, began to figure ways to raise money to pay for the big stained glass window that was to be placed on the front of the church, over the big double doors. Six smaller, colored glass windows would be set down each side of the church. A family could buy one small window and have their names put on it.

The ladies planned to make quilts and sell them over in Tennessee where they would bring more money than in the mountains. They got ten dollars and sometimes fifteen if the quilts were really pretty, or if some Yankee came by and bought one.

Things got to happening at B. J.'s place. The church house was going up built by men donating their labor. The ladies of the church brought dinner for workers.

Us boys fished and caught tadpoles in the creek that ran behind the old mill, and flirted with the pretty girls and pulled their pigtails. We'd run like Snider's pup so as not to get pointed out to our mamas. We knew they would dust the seat of our britches for such behavior.

Lord, my Mama liked to drove us crazy selling milk, butter and eggs. She'd run us over those ridges come rain or shine to sell fifty dollars worth to buy one of those small windows, just so she could see our name, Davis, written on it.

Well, the day came for us to hold services in the big, fancy church house on the hill. We had to don our best hand-me-downs, slick back our hair with bear grease and listen to our silly sisters fuss about who was going to sit on the front pews. I do believe the church felt as out of place as I did wearing John's hand-me-down britches. John got a new pair because there was no one to hand-him-down a pair. Mama made the girls little polka dot bows for their hair to wear with their speckled dresses. Mama told us boys no rock throwing for fear of breaking those pretty colored glass windows. We took heed because we had huffed across those mountains selling eggs and butter, and we thought twice about throwing rocks.

Some folks had a surrey to ride to church in, but my Dad was poor as old Job's turkey. We did have a big wagon, had to have to get all us young'uns in it. Old Bob and Red, the horses, were harnessed and ready to go that morning to church. I was proud myself of the church house, seeing how I'd helped with it. I'd just about wore my brogans out over those rocks and hills selling dairy products. We all got in the wagon and Dad hollered, "Giddy up" to the horses. They gave a yank and young'uns spilled out everywhere. When I bent over to help pull

97

Mary Jane back in the wagon, my britches ripped in the seat. I couldn't tell Mama. She was dying to get there on time. I took my coat off and tied it around me.

Mama said, " Will, why did you take your coat off ?"

I yelled back, "It cushions the blows when the wagon wheel hits a rock". That satisfied her. When we got to the church, I dodged her, and she never knew I'd ripped my britches until we got home.

All the ladies brought dinner which would be spread on the ground after the dedication service. B. J. had invited his friends from Snowbird to see the big church house. Mr. Fred Langford was our visiting preacher from Marble. We had no idea where Marble was, but he sure could tell about God and preached hell so hot you could feel the heat.

Mama invited him and Miss Grace, his wife, to spend Sunday evening with us so we all could come back to church that night. Fred and Grace came with the Rhodes family from Vengeance Creek in a surrey. They had to start out on Tuesday to arrive by Saturday in order to conduct the sermon on Sunday and to assist B.J. and Molly in the dedication service. They spent that night with B. J. and Molly.

We were the first wagonload to arrive at the new church house. We bailed out like onions rolling down a slope, anxious to take a look at the new church.

Mama said, "Now young'uns, first one I see misbehaving, I 'll take you out and thrash you like a bushel of oats." We sat still as church mice. We knew she'd do it.

Good folks were coming from everywhere: Marble, Murphy, Andrews, Robbinsville, Bryson City and one man said he'd rode a horse from Asheville. I bet his backside was in as bad a shape as mine with my ripped britches.

I couldn't wait for Fred Langford to stop his elegant preaching and get on with the dedication service to let us eat dinner. I could just taste my Grandma Dutch's fried apple pies and Bertha Mill's egg custards. The preacher ate more chicken and dumplings than I'd ever seen a preacher eat.

Mr. B. J. King and Molly, of course, got the honors of dedicating the new church house to God and B. J. King. Things went like clockwork up until one of B. J. and Molly's little brats throwed a rock and broke out the big colored glass window over the front doors. I figured what Miss Molly was about to do to him after church services ended. Lord, help their Claude and his rump when he got home.

We enjoyed Fred and Grace so much as they told about folk on Vengeance Creek. Fred and Grace stayed at B. J.'s that night and the Rhodes family stayed here and there with folks. We didn't have room for our brood, let alone company.

B. J. and Molly replaced the big window, but it didn't exactly match the color of the rest of the windows.

The fancy church house stood mocking the country mountains, but soon country ways gave in to uptown folk and the church house was more suitable for these different folks.

We all grew up, got jobs and left the Great Smoky Mountains for the city life. I longed for the mountains and the country way .

The big, fancy church house still stands and appears to make faces at the mountains, yearning, I guess, for the city as much as I yearned for the country.

God loves us one and all. He's always the same. It's people who mess up when they try to outdo their neighbors.

The Place of the Arrowheads

by Susan Broadhead

There is a place raised up amidst mountains,
a high meadow with creeks singing on all sides,
and the steep ridges rising beyond them
form a great bowl.

I go there to walk through tall grasses
filled with wild flowers according to their season
and it doesn't matter whether I am happy or sad
when the great round

of winter sky is filled with azure
and golden seed bracts gleam in the high poplars:
it is all one with spring's greening and the dogwoods
that border the field.

Here where a farmer named Paddy Flowers
once tilled the soil, I watch for places
where wild turkeys have scratched
the ground open,

and miraculously I find sharp points
of milky quartz made by a people long before us
who belonged to the earth in a way
we will never know.

But content or sorrowful, in that moment
I am connected with them through my
love of this place where they drank
from pure waters,

where they played in the tall grasses and knew
how to draw strength from root
and berry and flower--long ago,
when the power line

did not run through the gap between ridges,
when the trees were not dying
from acid rain--back when
the earth was eternal.

Funerals Are for The Living

by Mary E. Lynn Drew

Jim was cremated two days ago. It is for his wife, Althea, that I am here. I step out of the car for another memorial service wearing the dress I reserve for funerals. It is a gray, March day. I look over my shoulder at the sad graveyard packed with headstones and bouquets of plastic flowers.

I really hate to go to funerals. My grandmother went to all funerals. My mother would not go to any. I have stood bound in the middle between these two women all my life never finding a way to deal with this.

My grandmother's funeral outfit was all black–black hat, dress, gloves, shoes, umbrella. She went to funerals even when she didn't know the deceased. When asked why, she said, "I go for myself and I go for everybody else. Someone should be there to mark the day."

She never went to receptions. *Professional mourners* was the name for widow women who frequented funerals to eat at the receptions which followed.

I hesitate a moment as the church door opens. Brother Orlo welcomes me in and someone helps me to a pew.

When I was about four, Grandmother was keeping me on a day when she was to attend a large funeral. She dressed me up and took me with her. Once inside the darkness, we stopped and stood, then stepped again down the carpet-strip to the casket. There was lots to see on the way: there was carpet with a pattern, an enormously high ceiling with hanging lamps, dark, shiny wood and all kinds of feet. I stretched my neck up to see the coffin.

Grandmother peered into it a long time, then decided I was missing it all and picked me up to hold me over the corpse for a good look. Looking down at the body, I asked loudly, "Is he dead yet?" Like he was in process–in the oven–like death wasn't done all at once.

Mother learned later about my remark and was upset because Grandmother had taken me with her. In later years Mother sent me to her funerals. She never went. She sent me to her husband's and her son's funeral while she grieved at home.

I was eleven when my little brother drowned accidentally. The family never talked about his death. I sit in this new church today where Jim's service is being held. An old, oak screens the window near me. A plain, scarlet carpet leads to the stained glass pane behind the rail. I lean forward to pray and am aware of a low hum of voices undulating. A word now and then tells me that this hum is people comforting one another. More mourners enter pews. Family is bunched shoulder to shoulder in the first two rows ahead of me. Instead of praying, I ruminate.

It takes a year, I think, four seasons of remembering what you did together on holidays, his birthday, your birthday. It takes a year for the flesh to leave the bones and molder into dust leaving bones relaxed. A year is not always enough but custom says, *It has been a year, take off the armband, remove the veil.*

I look up. One tardy family member, a son, perhaps, or a nephew has joined the others. People rock to the center making room for him in the pew. He is hugged by a young woman who massages his shoulder. We stand for the prayer that begins the service. It is a prayer of cushioned words with comforting music in the background, the components of a funeral.

It was not these things that kept Mother away from funerals, it was the outward show of emotion. Grieving was a private experience. Mother was a Victorian lady, or at least the progeny of one, with a Victorian attitude. Even while having a baby, breaking a limb, or grieving she knew a display of emotions was not permitted in public. A widow was permitted to excuse herself from a dining table, a meeting or receiving line. She tended her grief and returned with dry though red eyes.

Our ways haven't changed much. We still believe in a facade. A friend said to me three months after her husband's death, "I went to a meeting. I thought I could handle it. But when the first person took my hand and said they were sorry, my face crumpled."

I have watched my friends say good-bye to a lifetime mate, and I think a great deal these days about my approaching death without fear of it as I did in my younger days. . .but I think about it. Mother thought about her mortality a lot. She changed her will regularly and added codicils often. I thought her behavior odd, that she must be depressed. In her later years it was nothing to have the yellow pages of the phone book fall open to a note, *In the event of my death. . .* Finding notes in phone books, dictionaries and calendars jarred me a time or two. She wasn't depressed, she was just thinking about it.

The music's volume increases and fades as the prayer ends and Brother Orlo remembers high points of Jim's life, as related to him by Althea and the children. I remember those of my family who are gone. I remember the first person I knew who died during my young life. Brother Orlo recounts Jim's experience in WW II, but my mind is on my father's grandmother, great-aunts and uncles, and another war. I remember a great-grandmother the shape of a little sack of pudding, aproned, dipping snuff, rocking on her weathered porch, blind.

She was attended by my great-aunts who led her off to wash supper dishes. The aunts, Mary and Martha, washed the dishes after she did but never told her. My great-grandmother was married at thirteen to a Union soldier, who was referred to by her family as *the northern gentleman*. They made no other mention of him but accepted her widow's war-pension checks that came. When Great-Grandmother died, our family lived too far to get to the funeral in time.

Someone coughs. I am aware that the minister is still on Jim's life as I recall Great Uncle Peyton, Great-Grandmother's son, who was a fireman in charge of the dray horses that pulled the fire wagons. When the fire bell rang, the strapping beasts stepped into their traces eager to be off down the streets of Petersburg. Those streets were flooded with Union troops less than ten years before the grandmother—who held me over the casket—was born in 1874.

God, I'm old. It hits me hard. I have held hands with, and have been kissed by, people who lived during the Civil War. I am old and entertaining thoughts during my friend's husband's memorial service. I wonder if any others here are thinking of a roast in the crock pot or a real estate closing.

I glance at Althea's stricken face. I came to remember Jim, but mostly I came to grieve with her, his wife. The oldest son stands to say a few words about his father. Tears flow on the family row. I see on the table facing them memorabilia, a photo of a smiling soldier. I wonder if Jim's cremains are on the table. I shove that borderline inappropriate thought aside.

Brother Orlo asks if anyone wishes to speak. Molly stands. She was a neighbor for twenty years back in Ohio. She tries to get her feelings out but breaks in the second sentence. Right here is where I begin weeping. I am fine one moment, dabbing my face the next.

I straighten up quickly when Brittany, Althea's small granddaughter, slips from the front pew taking pledge envelopes and a pencil with her.

She's dressed in a below-the-knee, white, crepe dress and white shoes and tights. She looks like a small angel moving down the aisle to the assistant minister's distant singing. Brittany scribbles a three-year-old's writing on the envelopes and delivers them up and down the aisles very respectfully.

Mourners smile when they accept the *letters*. When she finishes delivering mail (there are no more envelopes) she goes back to sit with her mother, daughter of the deceased. New tears flow. I dab. I look around. People are crying silently near me. I wonder if they are thinking what I am thinking, that when the little girl asked where Grandpa was she may have been told he was gone. And that is why she gave the sad people letters to send—and right there is where I stop. If I think about this I will have to leave the service.

Another of Jim's daughters is speaking. She describes the death bed scene. Jim died with family around him, and his arms around Althea. The daughter speaks calmly and hopefully.

I swing my knees to one side to let A.C. and Frances go past me. A.C. goes to the doctor every week. They did not know Jim or Althea until a month ago in the doctor's office. Frances sees me crying and she starts hearing the Hospice and Home Health nurses speak of how kind Jim was. One nurse tells of a dream. Jim was with God and God was hugging Jim.

We sing *How Great Thou Art*. Something in the moaning rise of the music speaks of deep grief.

I can feel Frances's tears. Is she thinking of A.C., her husband, sitting beside us, going to the doctor's office once a week? Is she wondering who will go first and how sad the one left will be? The whole church could be thinking of their loved ones' dying. Then I think about myself. Ollie, an in-law in Florida, is older than I am, but I could be next. I make a mental note to tell the kids that a memorial ceremony right away is not a good idea. They can handle it better later. I make another note to update my will. I haven't done that since I moved here. I could go any time. I am past the average age for women.

I don't want to see my daughter suffering. She gets a swollen face when she cries. I hate it when I think about this. First I am crying about Althea, then about my own loved ones who will be grieving for me. But they are young and healthy and active, so am I grieving for myself? How many here are grieving for themselves? I look at Frances. Her face is like my child's will be. And with that I change to practical thoughts.

In first place, in my natural scheme of things, are trees and rocks. I love trees and rocks. I will tell my children to transplant a young tree, a red oak I think, and fertilize its roots with my ashes. I see myself rise dramatically into this tree, extending my arms upward through its branches. My tree may die, in which case somebody had better plant another. Suddenly the music's volume increases with vibrato.

The family files out to stand at the back and receive us. One of Jim's sons announces a reception being held at the hotel.

"Everybody come. Please come," he says, pain swelling his voice.

I realize I am standing in front of Brother Orlo. I shake hands with him and say out of habit, "Enjoyed it."

I understand what I said and step back to grab his still outstretched hand.

"No–I didn't. Enjoy it!" And then. "You know what I mean."

His eyes dart about for a clue. When nothing comes, he looks me in the eye and says, "Amen."

Outside the sun bursts free and shines brightly for a moment, like it does sometimes after weddings and funerals. People will speak of that later. When I reach my car, I lick my right thumb, touch it to the center of my left palm and stamp the spot with the underside of my fist. I have no idea where that came from. It could have been a gesture dredged up from a childhood funeral settings; maybe coming home in the car afterward playing *license plates.* As I back the car out of the churchyard, I am thinking I had not done any better today, at the funeral, than I did at that first one with Grandmother.

I am suddenly reminded of a March day like this one when the sun blinked out and the world turned gray. The day was the funeral of my son-in-law's mother. We had not known his mother very long. He is a sincere person, my son-in-law. I thought he was controlling his emotions like the young men of his generation who were concerned with being *cool.* They received bad news with little show of emotion. That day in the limousine he had a helpless, bewildered look when he turned to me with a blank face, and said, "I don't know what I am supposed to feel."

I responded with a pat on his shoulder. It had not occurred to me that you had to have a feeling before you could grieve. I had supposed that feelings were all around, ready to be used.

As I turn on to the four-lane toward home, a headache settles across my brow. I put it away because I am still into revelations of this morning. It crosses my mind that during my life I have seen a lot of grief, and at this age I will see more. This seems to be a day of epiphany so I ponder the alternative to grieving. If there were no grief, could we measure joy? The headache reclaims my attention. My body is drained. I do not like to weep like this. Maybe I will stop attending funerals. Maybe. For awhile.

Good Friday

by Robin Taft Smith

I am splitting the remainder of our wood pile
this afternoon. It is April, and if the wood
weren't knotted and gnarled, we would have used
it by now. I have borrowed my neighbor's wedges
as this wood will not be split by maul alone.

Yesterday, Maundy Thursday, a hawk-like bird,
about the size of a crow, killed a dove in our yard.
My wife saw it as she drove up the driveway. She saw
it perched on the chopping block, the dove's neck
bent to the side in a death pose, and then it was off,
carried by wings powerful enough to lift a dove straight up,
over the wrought iron fence and out of sight. There is blood
and seeded feces on the chopping block and, everywhere,
feathers.

I think about the sound I'm making driving metal into wood,
a distinctive hammering of clank... clank... clank...
choking up on the sledge out of fatigue,
sometimes barely able to lift and strike the wedge
again and again. All afternoon, throughout
my neighborhood, Christ is crucified.
This ringing out must pain the believers.
I imagine them at their windows in anguish,
praying that I stop. And yet I continue
until I am so tired that I watch as a log teeters
and then falls on my shin.
Having failed to move, I too, bleed.

The Caney Creek Killing

by Jo Carolyn Beebe

On the morning of June 14, 1872, in the rural community of Caney Creek, Mississippi, nineteen-year-old Nathan Shannon was killed. Later that day his twin brother, Ethan, discovered his body and fell dead at the sight.

At their funeral, the preacher of Caney Creek Baptist Church read from The Bible about the mysterious ways of the Lord. He asked the question that was on everyone's mind: Why was Nathan killed? He was a poor boy on his way to the gold fields out west with nothing to reward a robber. Ethan's death was no mystery, of course. Everyone knew he had died of a broken heart when he saw Nathan's dead body. The Shannon tragedy had happened because Nathan got it in his mind to leave the family farm.

The boys' father, John Shannon, had returned from the War Between the States, a bitter man. His plantation had been confiscated, acre by acre, by scalawags until it could no longer be called a plantation. He was driven, bent on restoring what little land was left to him to the grandeur it had been before the war. Without slaves and unable to afford hired help, he worked his sons relentlessly. He was especially hard on Nathan who he considered his first born. Although Ethan was Nathan's twin, he had been the second baby to be born, and Shannon held with the old ways that the eldest son would be heir to the Shannon lands.

Nathan came to hate farm work. He hated the plowing and shoveling manure. He hated the uncertainty of the harvests. He hated the whiplashes he received from his father when he failed to get a job done on time. The tongue-lashings were nearly as bad as the beatings. But most of all, he hated his father's unrealistic attitude that things would be the same as they were before the war. And so it was that Nathan decided he would strike out on his own. He was not going to stay on the farm forever groveling in the fields, never knowing what it was like to be somebody. Somebody like Lawyer Price or Dr. Ballard or even Mr. Barnes who ran the mercantile.

He was anxious to tell Ethan about his plans. They had never kept secrets from each other. It occurred to him that this was the first time he had made a decision without Ethan. The boys grew up loving each other as twins do. They knew each other's thoughts, finished each other's sentences and often dreamed the same dreams.

On Saturday night, as they lay in bed, Nathan told Ethan he was leaving the farm. Ethan sat bolt upright in the bed he shared with his twin.

"Aw, Nathan. You can't mean that. You can't go so far away from me."

"I want you to come with me. We'll work our way west and when we get to the gold fields, we'll be rich."

"Papa won't let us leave. He'll beat the daylights out of us. And Mama will have the vapors. She'll cry and carry on and have to be dosed with her laudanum."

"Ethan, that's what I mean. Papa is either going to work me to death or beat me to death, and Mama is smothering me to death. I'm going to die if I stay here. We've got to get away."

"I can't. I'm scared. I can't forget what it was like when the Yankees burned us out. Don't you remember how hungry we got when we tried to get to Grandfather's?"

"We were eight years old. We know how to take care of ourselves now," Nathan said.

"But Mama, what about Mama? Ever since the Yankees came through here she does strange things."

Nathan interrupted. "Mama never had to make any decisions and when Papa was away fighting and the slaves all left, she lost her mind for a while."

Ethan said, "That's another reason for not leaving. Papa might turn on her if he don't have us to beat on."

"You know we can't live with Papa and Mama forever. We've talked about that. Getting married, having families of our own," Nathan said.

"Yeah, but we were going to get farms close together. We'd still see each other every day," Ethan said, panic in his voice.

"That was your idea. I never said I was going to stay here and farm."

"Nathan, I can't live here alone. I can't stand up to Papa like you can."

"Well, come with me. I don't know what it'll be like not being with you. I think it'll be like half of me has left but half of me is still here."

There was a long silence from Ethan's side of the bed. He lay back down and stared into the darkness. Through jerking sobs, the boy who had been taught that a man doesn't show his emotions by tears whispered, "You can't leave me, Nathan."

Nathan reached for his brother. Clasping his shoulder, he said, "Ethan, I'm going. I'm going to tell Papa tomorrow night. Please come with me."

The boys tossed and turned all night. Ethan dreamed that he was floating above a dark ravine, but he was not afraid for he could see Nathan and their old brown dog waiting there for him.

The next morning at breakfast, Nathan said to Ethan, "I had the strangest dream. I was in a hole or something, and you were floating above me looking at me." Ethan told him he'd had the same dream.

On Sunday night at the supper table, Nathan crumbled cornbread into his glass of buttermilk, then meticulously dabbed at crumbs that had fallen on his mama's only remaining linen tablecloth. Ethan watched Nathan and waited for him to make his announcement. Ethan ached for his twin, knowing how he dreaded telling Papa and Mama he was leaving home. Since the boys had slept very little the night before, their nerves were frayed and they were uncommonly quiet.

Lillian Shannon felt the tension between the boys and attempted to start a conversation by talking about their neighbors' plan to go west.

"What do you reckon they aim to do out there?" her husband asked.

"Well, the little boy has a notion to be a soldier and chase Indians," she laughed.

"Soldiering ain't no easy job," John Shannon said, remembering his experience in the infantry.

"Well, there's talk of the gold fields," Lillian said. "Whatever they do, I'm sure going to miss them when they go."

Nathan winced at his mama's remark but saw his opportunity.

"I'm going to try my luck out west, and I think a good time to leave would be next week. I've been saving my spending money to buy a train ticket, so I guess you need to know I'll be leaving next week and . . ." Nathan knew he was running off at the mouth, but he didn't want to stop and have to listen to what his parents were going to say.

Lillian's hands went to her mouth as she stifled, "My Lord."

John Shannon looked at Nathan, and Nathan met his stare.

"You a'going too, Ethan?" John Shannon almost shouted, never taking his eyes from Nathan.

"No, sir," Ethan whispered.

"Nathan, it appears you have been planning this for some time. Just how you planning on traveling?"

"I'm going to walk to Campbell Town, hitch a ride on the mail wagon to Tupelo and catch a train headed west."

"Ethan, how do you feel about this?"

"I'll miss him awful, and I don't want him to go, but I reckon we ought to let him. The sooner he goes, the sooner he'll come back."

Nathan darted a surly glance at his brother.

"You think I'll be back because I'll get homesick or something? I hate this farm. I'm never going to come back here to break my back plowing and shoveling manure. If'n I do come back, it'll be as a rich man. I'm going to be somebody!"

"Cussed boy!" John Shannon leaped up overturning his chair. "You know how much I depend on you. I fought my way out of hell to get back here to this farm. I bowed and scraped in front of the carpetbaggers to keep them from stealing the place. I am not going to let you get away with this half-witted plan of yours."

"Nathan," Lillian said. "I never expected such a thing from you. Do you think your papa is going to let you go off from here? Besides, you can't leave Ethan. Why, you've never been apart since the day you were born." She got up from the table and started stacking the dirty dishes.

"Nathan," she snapped, "throw these cornbread scraps out to the dog. Ethan, take the tablecloth outside and shake it." She walked into the kitchen and began to wash the dishes furiously. "How could Nathan do such a thing?" she mumbled to herself. They would be disgraced. She paused, holding a spoon suspended in midair, and looked up at the row of herbs and spices on an upper shelf. She smiled, then continued to slowly soap the plates and glasses.

John Shannon went to the mantle where his pipe lay, filled it with tobacco, and clamped the pipe stem hard between his teeth. He walked to the window and watched Nathan toss bread to the old brown dog that didn't have a name. The next week the farm work went on as usual. Each family member attended to his chores, Nathan working extra hard in order not to leave too much for Ethan and Papa to do.

On the following Monday morning, Nathan said good-bye to his mother and his brother. His father remained in the field plowing.

There had been few words between father and son during the past week. John Shannon watched the farewell scene at the house as he guided the plow along the straight rows where he would plant beans. Beans that Nathan had suggested would grow in the exhausted red clay fields overworked by years of cotton crops.

His mind was racing. "That boy thinks he ain't no farmer, but him and me could have the biggest harvests in these parts. Ethan loves the

111

land, but he don't know how to plan ahead. Nathan hadn't ought to have deserted me. Deserters don't get away free." A black scowl covered his face, and he jerked the reins so furiously that the mule stumbled and snorted at the unusual treatment.

On the other hand, Nathan's mother had fussed over him all week, cooking his favorite foods each day, washing and darning his clothes.

She was up earlier than usual on the day of his departure, clattering around in the kitchen making extra biscuits and sausage to pack in his valise for his lunch. She took a bottle of jimson weed from her spice shelf where she kept a supply of the weed for mixing with tallow to make salve for treating burns. When ingested, it caused nausea and delirium, and a large amount had been known to be fatal. The crushed weed resembled cayenne pepper used for seasoning sausage. She fried Nathan's sausage separately from the rest of the family's breakfast and sprinkled it liberally with the jimson weed. "After Nathan eats two or three of these sausage biscuits for lunch, he'll be too sick to travel and he'll come back home," she mumbled to herself.

When it was time for Nathan to leave, his mother clung to him and begged him to change his mind. She watched her boy walk out of her life as she stood weeping with Ethan.

Ethan had shaken his brother's hand and told him to take care of himself. A lump in his throat choked him, and he noticed Nathan also cleared his throat repeatedly. As Nathan turned away, Ethan grabbed him in a bear hug and again urged him not to leave him behind. Nathan's reply was the same as it had been all week, "Come with me." Ethan could only shrug and say, "I can't."

He watched Nathan and the old brown dog until they turned the corner at the end of the lane. Then he got his gun, stuffed two sausages and biscuits that he had sneaked out of Nathan's valise into his pocket and told his mama he was going to get a mess of quail. It would make everybody feel better about Nathan's leaving if they had a special noon meal, he had said.

He ran through the barn lot and climbed the rail fence. Swiping tears that trickled down his cheeks, he avoided the field where his father was working. He often hid in the woods when troubled, so he hurried along familiar paths hardly aware of the stinging slaps he was receiving from tangled shrubs and low branches.

When he came to the sagebrush patch, where the quail nested, he sank into the covering of the tall grass. His head slumped to his chest as he wept long racking sobs. After a while, the lump in his throat eased. The smell of his mother's sausages was comforting so he ate the food that was meant for his brother. Exhausted from his tearful siege, he alternately dozed and watched for his quarry. He gazed across the field and saw the sagebrush swaying in a sinuous dance. He was mesmerized as the grass parted to the left, then to the right, as quail leisurely zigzagged into the trees which closed around them, protecting them from their hunter. Ethan picked up his gun and crept toward the movement. The trees shifted and blocked his vision. He felt giddy and stumbled every few feet. A wave of nausea caused him to lower his weapon and drop to his knees. Perspiration drenched him, and he was suddenly overcome with anxiety. Something evil was just beyond the trees.

Nathan and the dog had been walking for three-quarters of an hour when the dog turned toward the woods that bordered the road. He stared into the undergrowth, then began to wag his tail. Nathan joined the dog, peering into the foliage.

"What 'cha see, boy?"

The shotgun blast exploded Nathan's chest. The impact lifted him off his feet and hurled him across the road into the roadside gully. He was dead by the time his body came to rest in the bed of dust.

The dog ran from the noise, but when the echo passed, he looked back anxiously for Nathan. He watched as a shadow appeared from the woods.

"Come here, boy."

Ethan picked up Nathan's valise and moved to the shade at the edge of the woods. Opening the satchel, he removed the sausage biscuits that his mother had prepared for Nathan's journey.

"No need to waste good food," he called to the dog. "I done ate two of Nathan's sausages. Might as well finish 'em since he left them just laying here by the road. Wonder why he dropped his valise."

The old dog approached the familiar, yet suddenly sinister, figure with caution, his tail tucked in submission. When he reached the gully, he looked down at Nathan's body. He jumped into the ditch and nuzzled his master.

Ethan leaned against a black gum tree as he ate the sausage and biscuits and hummed a nonsensical tune. After eating the sausages, his heart began to race. There was a pounding in his temples. His inner ears were ringing. His legs and arms felt heavy, and he had difficulty rising to his feet. He shuffled to the edge of the gully and looked at the crumpled form lying in red blood mingled with red dust. He saw his curly hair, his nose, his mouth, his eyes staring up at him. He gasped as pain crushed his ribs. He placed a hand on his chest expecting to feel the moisture of his blood. But his chest was not bleeding. The chest in the ditch was bleeding.

"Nathan-n-n-n!" he screamed.

Ethan felt himself begin to float above Nathan and the old brown dog. The dog jumped aside when Ethan's body tumbled into the ditch and came to rest on top of his brother. The dog licked the identical faces of the twins and whined.

Brush Pile

by Kathleen M. Crisp

At last, a day with rain.
Time to burn accumulated brush.

Privet's gone for red azaleas,
man slings out old for new.

Splintered pines from stormy winds,
lay like a shattered heart.

Ancient holly bushes scrawny,
prickle as they creak and crake.

Flames vault high ,orange, black
and yellow mingle. Blue grey
smoke announces
the location of my fire.

Who'll roast marshmallows
in the vapors of my memory?

Are Scouts from childhood days,
or, fishermen who camped

in old-time days ready
to ghost up above

the ashes
of my dying brush pile?

Gypsy Grandmother

by Ramona Layne Stylos

I still miss my gypsy grandmother sometimes, but not as much as I did decades ago when I was fourteen. Maybe fourteen is the worst possible age to lose one of your favorite relatives or your soul mate and especially someone who is both. I never really met my gypsy grandmother and, in fact, she wasn't actually my grandmother. She lived much too early for that. My mother liked to refer to her as *one of my foremothers*, and since I didn't have a real grandmother as I was growing up, I decided quite early that Gypsy Lena–as the older relatives called her–could take the place of my grandmothers. More like a fairy godmother. I talked to her in my mind and felt like she was listening. She seemed able to make things happen that I really needed to happen.

I always liked the idea that there was a gypsy in the family, though I had never seen any gypsies that I knew of. When I was growing up, gypsy caravans no longer passed through, stopping for a time down near the creek, then moving on. And parents no longer warned their children of the dark-skinned people with gold earrings who would carry off a child if the child wandered too far from home. All that belonged to the time of my parents' childhood.

I was about twelve, maybe thirteen, the first time I heard gypsy music. It was in a movie. There was a part about gypsies who lived and sang and danced as they did generations ago, and I was totally entranced by it. The music moved me as no music ever had. More than the country music my parents liked to listen to, and more than the Hit Parade music I listened to with my friends on Saturday night. It was like something I almost remembered, and it stirred in me a great sadness and longing for something I couldn't imagine.

I remember the moment the idea flashed into my head: Of course! I loved this music because I had gypsy blood in me! And Gypsy Lena and I must have a special bond! The idea excited me but not in a way that made me want to talk to anybody about it. I walked, instead, around the far part of the orchard where the damson plum trees grew and thought about my new discovery. I imagined that if the gypsies were still around, they would like this place at the edge of the orchard. They might have rested their caravans here for awhile.

After that I spent hours in the library reading books about gypsies. There were some novels, all old with brittle pages. People didn't seem to be writing stories about gypsies anymore, but there were some non-fiction books. I devoured them all. I learned how the gypsy king was chosen; I read stories passed down through generations about *unexplainable happenings,* and learned how important the moon, especially the full moon, has always been to the gypsies.

"Me too," I wanted to say to somebody. I love the moon, and things *are* different during the full moon. I have felt it. Someday, I imagined, there would be someone I could say such things to.

No one in our family talked about that part of our ancestry so I kept my interest in Gypsy Lena to myself. Then one day I really wanted more information, so I asked my mother.

"What kind of gypsy was my gypsy grandmother? Was she Hungarian or Spanish or something else?" I remember my mother looking at me funny to see if I was really serious. Of course I was.

"You mean Gypsy Lena? Well, she wasn't really your grandmother, you know." Yes, I did know. She was my mother's great-aunt. So, of course, she wasn't really a gypsy, just plain old Scotch-Irish like the rest of us. She said that in an off-handed way, as if it didn't really matter. People called her a gypsy because she never stayed home. She was a real *traipsing woman,* always on the go. They say she rode a horse from North Carolina to Kentucky before there was a road over the mountains.

I think she went on to say something about how this early liberated woman could shoot as good as any man, but I had quit listening. I didn't want to believe it. It couldn't be true! Gypsy Lena didn't live in a caravan or tell fortunes or wear gold hoops in her ears! I couldn't let Mama know how devastating this new information was for me. At first I felt furious at her for telling me. I wanted to smash the phonograph records of gypsy music I had been collecting. *That mournful music,* as my friends called it. But, of course, I couldn't because more than just mad, I was grief-stricken and sadder than I had ever been.

I couldn't accept the idea that Gypsy Lena wasn't really a gypsy and that I had no gypsy blood in me at all. I mourned and moped and listened to my sad records. At least there was one person capable of understanding the grief I was feeling. It was that whoever could make the gypsy violin cry like that! That helped a little.

117

That was years ago, and eventually I became used to the idea that I was not part gypsy, not even a little bit. Well, most of the time I have accepted it. But, sometimes in the early spring, or late Indian summer and especially on the nights of the full moon, I remember something I used to know but then forgot: something sweet and wild and compelling. Something that tells me, but not in words, that facts aren't everything, that there are, indeed, *unexplainable happenings.*

Ivory Combs

by Kathryn Stripling Byer

He sat on the porch every morning
and dreamed he would someday go wandering farther
than all he could see beyond Burning Wing Gap.
"Hear the wind," he sighed.
"Just like a woman she never stops calling me."

"What does she say?" I teased.
"That you're a cold-hearted man who cares more
for his rambling than for any wife?"

How he laughed!
Then he straightened his hat
and tried hard to look solemn.
"That song you sing when you turn sad,
Oh, it's down, down went her ivory combs,
sing it now," he said,
pulling me onto his lap.

I untangled his hands from my waist
and stood up again, smoothing my apron,
for I had grown tired of the old songs,
their garlands of rue and their thorny vines.
So many winding sheets.

I walked away to the edge of the apple trees,
watching him over my shoulder.
I let down my hair,
and he took off his hat,
tossed it far as he could in the sunlight.
The shady grass lay like a promise between us,
concealing the first of its gay wings
and meadow-sweet. "Gypsy girl,"
I heard him calling.
I watched him come after me,
crushing the wildflowers under his feet.

119

Kathleen's Wedding

by Nita Gilbert

Kathleen burst through the door of the kitchen, briskly walking to the bulletin board and expertly eyeing the menu.

"Tipsy," she called out. "Grab three rolls of hamburger."

Tipsy, a tall black man, headed for the freezer grabbing three five-pound rolls of meat.

"Shannon, nineteen bowls of potatoes."

Shannon grabbed a steel pan and placed it in the sink. Hastening to the pantry, she gathered small red potatoes and hurrying to the sink she measured them out into the pan.

"Terri, you're on salad," and Terri ambled slowly to the cooler, poking at things green and round. Gradually she pulled out handfuls of radishes, onions, lettuce, tomatoes, bell peppers, and carrots, all of which she placed on a cart and rolled it to the stainless steel, double sink where she liked to work alone with her thoughts.

Kathleen was the supervisor and chief cook at the John C. Campbell Folk School in Brasstown, North Carolina. This is where she had worked since she was a young girl. The school was known for teaching people across the nation and around the world country arts such as weaving, blacksmithing, rug making, quilting and pottery.

Standing alone at her workstation, Kathleen mixed sixteen cups of wheat flour with eight cups of white flour into a huge mixing bowl for the nightly bread. A variety of bread was baked fresh several times weekly for the stayover students and visiting teachers. The yeast rose aromatically as Kathleen dusted the stainless steel table in front of her, as well as her rolling pin preparing to hand-knead and roll out the twenty loaves she was about to bake in the two industrial upper level ovens. The kitchen sure felt homey when bread was baking.

"Shannon, Teri, Tipsy! Y'all listen up. We have to hurry. Tonight's a wedding reception! Ninety-five people they said, from nine to midnight. Somebody's getting married and celebrating it here!"

Kathleen grinned with pride like a mother enumerating the wonderful traits of her children. She was very proud of the folk school dining hall, as she had watched it grow from a tiny, two-room affair attached to the back of a studio to the large room of shining paneling, wood trim, and polished wood flooring. From the street, in the evening, the dining hall lit up with a warm and inviting glow that enticed people to come in.

Tipsy moaned. He was known for his certain addictions, and the thought that he might not get to indulge them this Saturday night, disrupted his peaceful state. He grunted and frowned pursing his lips, but Kathleen ignored him. She needed his muscles for the moving and arranging of the wooden tables in the main dining hall, and the lifting of the heavy chairs afterwards.

Terri spun another tale about her sick baby whose childhood illnesses coincided perfectly with her distaste of whatever project was at hand. If a pediatrician, and not Kathleen, had been diagnosing, her child would be in an intensive care unit in a hospital somewhere having extensive examinations, both internally and externally. Kathleen rolled her eyes but relented as always allowing Teri to leave right after dinner was served and the plates put away. Kathleen favored the coffee-colored, slightly-built child with the brownish amber eyes so magically lit and large, with eyelashes curling back like a doll's. She granted Teri favors for his sake.

Shannon just nodded acceptance, knowing she had no family or excuse to leave early. She often covered for the infirmities and emergencies of Teri and Tipsy.

At precisely 6:00 p.m. the school hostess clanged the large dinner bell on the dining hall porch. Shannon rushed over to Kathleen.

"The tea is still hot, Kathleen!"

"Put it on the drink table," Kathleen said, "They're coming in."

Folks hustled down the tree-shaded sidewalks briskly scurrying for the final meal of the day. Tonight it consisted of meatloaf with whipped potatoes and gravy, fresh bread, vegetables, salad and Texas brownies for dessert. Students and teachers filed in singly, pouring hot tea into ice-filled glasses and hastened to their seats for the quick prayer of grace and thanks to the Maker who had shed His abundance of homegrown food, good teaching, and friendly folks so graciously on the school's grounds. The bowls began rapidly changing hands amidst the clamour of laughter and quick-witted jibes of rustic humour.

Dinner was over, the coffee drunk and the plates were placed onto the stainless steel lazy susan. Tipsy quickly washed the food from the plates before placing them in the industrial dishwasher. Washing dishes was Tipsy's favorite job in the kitchen.

The bride's caterers moved in with their plastic *crystal* punch bowls and sterno roasting pans full of fresh vegetables and meats. Melons cut into picnic baskets with jagged-edged handles were filled with small, round melon balls and grapes. It was a beautiful reminder of spring and the abundance of life.

At precisely 9:00 p.m., the wedding party arrived. Young girls in slinky material moved into the room in a group waving their corsaged wrists in conversation awash with giggles. They eyed the young men in ill-fitting pants with flirtations looks as the men sashayed in like so many peacocks, courting feathers spread for attention. Some young men headed to the punch bowl knowing that everyone would be thirsty sooner or later, and especially the girls eager for a date. Others streamed silently to the balcony outside to sneak a smoke in the balmy night before the festivities began.

An elegant, older gentleman slowly entered the room, surveying his surroundings with darting glances, neither completely comfortable nor familiar with the young folks surrounding him. He sat stiffly among the clamor and laughter and stared fixedly at the back door awaiting his daughter's entry.

Soon the newlyweds entered the room, bending to the right and left to reach hands extended to them and smiling as cameras flashed like summer lightning. The band began a soft, slow tune that caressed the couple like a gentle blessing.

The proud father rose and went to his daughter's side, gently taking her hand then leading her with a slow swirl onto the dance floor where they danced. Kathleen sank slowly into a wooden chair in the smaller dining room. Her eyes fixed on the father and daughter like a hawk as they glided together around the edges of the dance floor closest to her.

Within minutes, the groom eased his way to his bride's side. He slid his arm around her small waist moving her from his father-in-law's grasp into a new dance rhythm even as her life would now be new at his side. The music and their moves flowed flawlessly.

"They make a most elegant couple," Shannon said.

Kathleen swayed to the left with the bride and then to the right, imitating the couple swirling so gracefully before her. Kathleen was transfixed by their twirling as the music moved them both in harmony.

As she sat there watching, she held her coffee cup high as if her hand was resting on someone's shoulders and she sighed, eyes closed, dreamily moving in a silent waltz.

"I never had parties," she spoke wistfully. "Married at sixteen and boom! Just like that. One, two, three babies in a row. It's never been easy. Never had pretty dresses like that," and she sighed, following the dancing bride with a twinge of envy in her eyes. The groom smiled as the couple swung past. Kathleen smiled back, as if she had a secret and that it was she and not someone else who was the newlywed bride.

Shannon, who had known better times than being a cook, and who had lived other places more elegant then her present surroundings, listened, her heart breaking for her friend, Kathleen, who had known nothing but work all her life, both here and at home.

To Shannon, Kathleen was a *woodsy* and it was the way of *woodsies* some of whom peopled the lush mountains around, to marry young. Shannon knew these people worked hard, played hard, loved consistently and died with the expectation of better times and places.

She knew Kathleen worked hard and would die late in years surrounded by many loving children and grandchildren, and, if it were possible to make her own funeral dress prior to that notable day of passing, she would do that too.

At 1:00 a.m., when the party was over, Kathleen and Shannon said their goodnights in the hot, humid parking lot where the dampness of the North Carolina spring literally dripped from the air. Shannon caught a glance of an unusual movement in the side mirror of her car and looked back.

Kathleen, swooping and twirling, tore her apron from her waist and flung it in a graceful arc over her shoulder into the backseat. As tired as she was, she seemed to float into her Ford truck. She wasn't a cook or even a mama anymore. She was into her dream world in another land and in another time.

Shannon smiled when she saw her drive by for she knew that no matter how tired Kathleen must have felt that night, her spirit was soaring free, dancing and twirling like a sixteen-year-old in a white dress with an orchid wristband, no babies on her hips, floating in the arms of a handsome young knight. The flour on her cheeks was the kisses of a new beginning, and her Ford the only steed she needed to ride into her future.

Shannon laughed to herself, thinking, *No doubt there'd be wedding punch on the menu tomorrow night. You just wait and see!* Then Shannon, too, shifted into first and drove slowly home on the curving mountainous roads thinking of the past and the future and wondering if there had ever been anything more magical in this world than new beginnings. She prayed for the newly-wed couple that they would never see the despair of divorce or know the pain of a lost child and hoped they would always remember that glorious moment of dancing for the first time as newly-weds. She had a feeling of truth in her heart that they would always swirl and sway and dance together, a most elegant couple, as the winds of the winds of life wafted them forward in time.

Surveying Trillium

by Mildred W. Greear

Where trillium grows, we walk the line
To see if it is his, or mine.
Sessile abundant; nodding, rare,
And property rights being what they are,

I search above to measure sky
To judge on whose side which may lie
And hope an arc of some degree
Declares they all belong to me.

Less comfort lies in clouds that shift
Than in the leaves that form a drift
Of cover bracing trillium stem
Which says but few belong to him.

A need to put all science by
In service to my greedy eye
Informs my very careful foot
To move respecting every root

Which curves from the surveying rod
To lose itself in mossy sod,
Erasing angles as one should
That cut through trillium in the wood.

Detours

by Carol Crawford

The machine shines on the shelf, full of inner broodings. I balance my weight on both feet, approach it alone and as an equal.

It's a bluff.

The thing makes me think of the Borg...some kind of twenty-fourth century gargoyle. I'm here to master it, to make it exhale steam on command and produce a trendy, fragrant beverage. I'm hostage, though, a balky participant in an odd epicurean ritual.

Len putters in the kitchen, wrangling food for the day. He clangs a lid. People hustle by the shop window, getting their exercise. The *Open* sign is dull, unlit, but still I worry. Sometimes they come in anyway.

I remove the filter basket from its place and slide it into the coffee dispenser. Two clicks of the handle fill the basket, and I catch the first heady whiff of espresso bean. I tamp it, flick the gritty excess off the edge, and ratchet the filter into place. With the press of a button the hum begins —a washing machine on spin. Scalding topaz trickles into a small pitcher and the aroma grows rich and comforting. It crosses my mind that the smell might draw people in too soon.

I hear Len's footsteps approach, hesitate and wisely turn away. "Yes," I had said six months ago. Go ahead, open a coffee store, meaning *him*. *He* could deal with the chrome, caffeine ogre. But we have been plagued with a sudden shortage of help, and here I am. I take milk from the refrigerator under the counter, pour it into a sleek stainless steel pitcher. I turn the knob for the steam wand to clear excess moisture. It hisses with dragonish menace.

The wand scorches my fingers. I nudge it forward with a thumbnail and dunk it just under the surface of the milk. It whooshes, churning foam. I submerge it farther.

When the bottom of the pitcher is almost too hot to touch, I pour the milk into a glass, holding back froth with a spatula. Next I scoot foam over the edge and pour espresso down the middle. Dust it with cinnamon.

The liquids dance, shifting and settling, testing each others' heft. Airy foam floats at the top...featherweight crown. The steamed milk is tinted ecru by espresso passing through to lurk in a bitter circle on the bottom. I assay the color, the depth of foam. Was this the way they looked in Atlanta the day we went from Starbucks to Barneys to Borders?

The taste is stout—vehement coffee, mollified only a little by the milk. Foam clings to my upper lip—ephemeral mustache. So much attention to a drink that would be gone in five minutes. Well, fifteen if it were accessory to a good conversation.

This was not my idea. Not my dream. I have dreams, lots of them. Aspirations including traveler, teacher, writer, speaker, bookstore owner. Some have been fulfilled, some not. But java merchant is not among them. What brought me to the point where all my faculties are focused on selling steamy twelve ounce cups to people I don't know in a place I don't belong? How did I get here, anyway?

When we announced we were moving a thousand miles to open a gourmet store in a hamburger town, reactions ranged from outrage to incredulity at Len's foolishness and my going along. I received odd, misplaced praise for being something I am not, and never have been a submissive wife. The move was not about submission. It was about choices, past and present. The choice to love and to continue loving in the face of change, loss and unexpected labors.

A man comes through the door, takes off his hat. A tourist?

"Hi," I greet him.

"Hey," he replies. A local, then. We discuss the weather for awhile.

"Would you like a cup of coffee this morning?" I ask him.

"Cappuccino," he says. He seats himself and watches me work the machine.

Home from a gauntlet of tiresome errands, I pull in the driveway and feel my shoulders unclench. My three daughters burst from the side door of the van like biscuits popping out of the can. I yell at them to take their book bags in, but they're already out and gamboling through the woods that surround the house, reveling in their freedom from the confines of the school day. I do not have the heart to call them back, but neither have I any intention of joining them. The day is rainy and cool. I'll go inside, make a fire, brew a cup of tea and glance at the paper before tackling dinner.

But they're back. Brilliant blue eyes alight and voices urgent, they inform me that I *have* to come with them, out under the trees, and I have to come *now*! My hands are full and so they tug at my elbows and the edge of my coat. They have found something special, they declare, something rare. The dogs scamper around us, tongues out, wagging their rear ends in the contagion of excitement.

I'm conquered. I step in the house just long enough to dump the purse, the bags from the drug store and the office supply, the sheaf of mail and the clothes picked up from the cleaners. Outside again, the moisture in the air is like a soft-focus lens, dulling sharp edges and adding a layer of gray to the greens of early spring. Trees lean out to touch needly fingertips over my head as I walk down the gravel drive. I am trying to befriend the trees but being prairie-bred, I long for openness and space. For a great quantity of air with nothing in it but sunshine. For a clear white light without a trace of fog. Such space is not to be found here even on the best of days, and my unexpected reluctance to embrace this particular landscape has made me wonder if I'll ever feel at home.

The girls have run on, ducking and darting through the limbs. I plod behind, getting rained on, thinking how my hair will frizz. Our umbrella was broken weeks ago, and I have never had the presence of mind to replace it. Once under the canopy of leaf and branch it doesn't matter. There wouldn't be room to open it, and the trees slow the torrent to a drippy-faucet pace. The moldy smell of ancient leaves wafts up to me as I crush the forest floor underfoot. I can see Abby's bright raincoat bobbing through the brush, then Emily's, then Caroline's. A plastic-clad arm motions, impatiently waving me forward.

My daughters reach the sacred spot and form a semi-circle around an insignificant-looking patch of ground. The old arthritic dog merely sniffs, but the younger one, infected by their delight, plunges into the middle of the group. The girls screech and grab her collar, pulling her away. She is one of those thick-chested, big-footed country dogs, and she is about to place her rump square upon a miracle.

It is a lady slipper.

We could so easily have missed it. It's hiding well away from the road, apart from the paths beaten by children's feet from fort to swing to treehouse. It is the palest of pinks, its bloom so fragile it seems to tremble at the end of the swan-neck stem.

Where I come from the flowers come out and declare themselves. Texas bluebonnets aren't shy. They fling themselves over the wide landscape like a cloth on the dining room table, announcing a special occasion: spring. I am not used to delicate introverts who hide among the towering trees and wait to be discovered. This is something new for us, something exotic. We kneel and admire the wildflower, mindless of mud and the passing of time. We talk about the softness of the leaves, the translucency of the petals, and our good fortune to have noticed it. The tea and the fire go unmade, the dinner is late, and it is all right. I carry the image with me all through washing up and bedtime stories. It is night, and they are all asleep before I realize I will have to thank the girls for the detour.

When I first met Len I didn't like him. He loves sports, I love Shakespeare. He is practical and straightforward and literal. When I explain a poem to him, with its intricate use of language and layers of meaning, he responds, "Well, why didn't they just say so?" We had one uncomfortable date after which we ditched the romance, kept the friendship.

But romance is a sneaky thing. It thrives best while you're not watching. There was something courtly in the way he'd call, asking me to reserve an hour to take a walk with him. In another time and place he might have been asking for a spot on my dance card. On those walks we discussed our troubles: with work, with roommates, with money. Confidences breed intimacy and intimacy breeds, all unexpected, love.

Because of love I have taken the most outrageous detour of my life and moved to the place Len grew up. It's a remote corner of the Georgia mountains, a town too small for a Wal-Mart.

Vacationing friends come to visit and Len tours them around. He tells them about the night that he and his cousins and uncles fanned over a certain ridge, trying to find a cow and her new calf before snowfall. He shows them a waterfall tucked away in the national forest a short drive from our house, a pocket of a park in a river bend, a bubbling spring he played in as a boy. Every stone and stream and rut in the road has a story, and as he tells that story, he shines.

He is obviously happy here, a fish back in water. I am prickly, dissatisfied. I listen to the locals like him who are bound to this place in some mysterious, psychic way. They will forego convenience, higher-paying jobs and all the other accoutrements of the city so that they can wake up every morning within sight of Big Frog Mountain. Some of the tourists are like that too. They come for a weekend and come back to retire. They want to spend the rest of their lives amid this landscape that, they say, speaks to them.

But it does more than speak. These old hills sing comfort and calm to those who can hear. Because I am tone-deaf to this particular music, Len has to translate for me, the way I translate poems for him. I agree Big Frog is beautiful, but it has no pull for me. Because it has no strings on my heart yet, I could leave it without a wrench. What pulls me is the city with its hectic energy, its bookstores and libraries and lights.

The place we have settled is too small even for streetlights, and this has disconcerted me from the first. In Dallas darkness meant danger. Any corner of shadow could conceal a thief or worse. We flooded our backyards with spotlights thinking to discourage burglary and vandalism. It mostly worked. I was never afraid of the dark because there wasn't any to speak of.

But when night falls in Epworth, Georgia, it is good and truly dark. It's rare to find a criminal waiting in the woods. The absence of illuminations spawns, instead, a wonder. It begins just at dusk with a wink here and there in the corner of your eye so brief you think you have imagined it. By bedtime the woods glitter like stars. The brush that crowds me so plays host to an astounding profusion of fireflies. They particularly like the obnoxious vine, kudzu, and hover over a field of it like so many fairy lights. There were lightning bugs in Texas, of course, but I have never seen them like this. They make me think of Christmas, of luminaria. Of magic.

We form the habit of gathering at my bedroom window before the girls go to bed, turning off all the lamps, and watching. It has rained earlier and there is no moon, so the display is particularly brilliant on this night. I've heard that fireflies communicate by means of their on-and-off glow. I mention this to the children and they take to the idea. They scatter to their beds, speculating about a sort of buggy Morse code. A voice floats back to me down the hall.

"But what in the world would a bug have to *say*?"

Sometimes, in the summer, I drive the kids back to Texas for a visit. Long trips with the family have a tendency to turn into marathons of endurance. We are too close together, cannot shift in our seats without rubbing elbows, cannot eat a snack without getting crumbs on someone else's magazine. Before we are even an hour away from the house, someone has the urgent need for a bathroom. Each flick of the air conditioning switch brings triple complaints: one child is too hot, one too cold, and one doesn't like the air in her face.

When a *Detour* sign rises up in the midst of the journey, I am more than put out. I am exasperated. Offended. Why wasn't I told about this? I pay my AAA dues every year, and this was nowhere on my triptych. The authoritative arrow points *away* from the main thoroughfare, the one I want to travel. I study the white-lined concrete stretching away into the distance, a sturdy band of gray, belting the earth. It looks solid, finished, as though it knows where it is going.

Then I turn my attention to the side route indicated by the arrow. Mere asphalt. It seems temporary, like an afterthought. It distinctly does not look like something that will get me to my intended destination. I pull onto the shoulder, put the car in park, let it idle.

The children squirm in the back. I do not dare delay my decision too long, or voice my fears out loud. Any obvious lack of confidence on my part brings on the dreaded, droning queries, more maddening than mosquitoes whining at your ear: "Are we lost?" "How much farther?" and "When will we get there?"

I pull out my reading glasses, glance at the map. The road I *want* to take, the one forbidden me, is a solid blue line, substantial, sure of itself. The detour, as near as I can figure, is a little string of blue dots. I look closer and I still can't make out where, precisely, I will get back on the highway.

I glower at the sign, then at the asphalt. Will there be bathrooms if I go that way? McDonald's? Roadside parks? Will there be a place to telephone, should I have car trouble? What will the scenery be like? I glance at the gas gauge, wondering when I'll have a chance to fill up again. Peer down the main road. There's no sign of construction or flooding, no bridges out or trees down as far as I can see. What could be so wrong with it that the highway department is directing me away?

Grumblings arise behind me, as though the girls have picked up my consternation.

"She got marker on me!"

"She was in my way!"

"That's *my* coloring book!"

I settle the artists' dispute, turn back to the wheel.

"Mom, why are we stopped?" I hear the edge of worry creep into the young voice.

"Just checking something," I say, with far more aplomb than I feel.

The sun hovers at half-mast; only a few hours remain before dark. I put the map aside for now, fold up the triptych, and pull onto the asphalt road. There will be–there must be–more signs farther ahead, some ken to tell me I've done the right thing, some symbol to show me the rest of the way.

April Rain

by Nancy Simpson

In memory of my father
who loved to sit on a covered porch
and watch rain, I sit sheltered
and sip coffee on my covered deck
high on Cherry Mountain.
Near treetops I sing louder than
the downpour that falls inches from me.
"You like my new house?" I trill
above the spill of raindrops.

Mr. Whiskers asleep on my feet
under the wicker seat, wakes.
He thinks my song is for him.
I look deep into gray mist, eye to eye
with thin green leaves of a thousand trees
and sing welcome to white blossoms
on dogwood trees no one planted.
I am singing. I am singing to my father
who loved to sit close to rain.

Over Mountains

by Emily Elizabeth Wilson

The mountains have folded over,
overlapping, overwhelming,
over words,
over silence,
quick drawing silence,
water colored layers
drying deeper
hues of purple
held ocean,
molded waves,
deep reefs of time.

Morning advises
a slow stance,
a quiet
still moment
as sun reaches its fingers
over the edge,
over time,
holding the light.

Biographical Notes:

Richard Argo, Murphy, NC, hails from Tampa, Florida. He is retired from the United States Coast Guard and is a graduate of the Evergreen State College. He settled in western North Carolina with his wife, Judy, where he writes prose and where they are building their home. Both writing and building, he says, progress slowly.

Barbara C. Arnold, Blairsville, GA, graduated from Massachusetts College of Art, Boston, Mass. She returned to Massachusetts College of Art for a B. S. degree in Art Education. Barbara moved to northern Georgia in 1990. She is a member of a critique and writing group in Young Harris, GA.

Glenda Barrett, Hiawassee, GA, is an artist and a writer of poems and essays. Her work has been published in *Georgia Magazine, Grit Magazine, Hearing Health Magazine, Whispers from Heaven Magazine, Mountain Lynx, Tri-County Communicator* and local newspapers.

Glenda Beall, Hayesville, NC, lives with her husband, Barry, and a dog named Rocky. She grew up in south Georgia and moved to the mountains in 1995. Her poems have been published in *The Journal of Kentucky Studies, Main Street Rag* and *Appalachian Heritage.*

Jo Carolyn Beebe, Hiawassee, GA, bases most of her stories on oral family history learned in north Mississippi. She has been published in *Lonzie's Fried Chicken* and *Heroes from Hackland.* Abingdon Press purchased a story based on her experiences as Director of Christian Education in Ohio.

Susan Broadhead, Franklin, NC, has lived in the mountains for eight years. Formerly the director of the Loft Literary Center in Minnesota, she now owns a company that builds traditional timber frame homes and barns. Her poems have been published in *Milkweed Chronicle* and *North Stone Review.*

Margaret Lynn Brown, *Brevard,* NC, teaches U. S. history at Brevard College and is the author of *The Wild East: a Biography of the Great Smoky Mountains.* She has published widely as a non-fiction author, but there are some stories, such as "Those Smoky Bears" that find their best form in a storyteller's voice.

Alma Stiles Bryson, Franklin, NC, is the fifth child of George and Agnes Angel Stiles. She was born and raised in Macon County. She was educated in public schools and earned a bachelor's and master's degree from W. C. U. While a widow, she raised four children. She taught school for twenty years.

Kathryn Stripling Byer of Cullowhee, North Carolina chose the poems for this anthology. She has taught at Western Carolina University for many years and is the author of *Girl in the Midst of the Harvest (Texas Tech Press), Wildwood Flower, Black Shawl* and *Catching Light,* (LSU Press). Her fifth book, *Coming to Rest,* is due in 2005. Kathryn received the Lamont Poetry prize from the Academy of American Poets and received The 2001 North Carolina Award in Literature.

Kenneth Chamlee, Brevard, NC, is a Professor of English at Brevard College. His poems have appeared in the *Asheville Poetry Review, The Cumberland Poetry Review, The Greensboro Review, GSU Review,* and other magazines. He has published two chapbooks: *Absolute Faith* (ByLind Press) and *Logic of the Lost (Longleaf Press).*

Carol Crawford, Blue Ridge, GA, has had poetry, fiction, and nonfiction published in *The Atlanta Journal–Constitution, The Chattahoochee Review, the Southern Humanities Review, The Dancing Shadow Review, the Journal of Kentucky Studies,* and others.

Helen N. Crisp, Canton, NC, grew up in Waynesville, NC. She is a graduate of Berea College, KY, and a retired hospital finance officer. Her poems have been published in *Sunburst, Manna, The Wayah Review, The Atahita Journal* and in one of the National and The International Library of Poetry books.

Kathleen Crisp, Andrews, NC, retired from Social Services. She has found writing poetry absorbing. Her poems have been published in *Bay Leaves, Main Street Rag, Lone Wolf Review, Laurels* and several anthologies.

Thomas Rain Crowe, Tuckaseegee, NC, is a poet, translator, editor, publisher, recording artist and author of eleven books of original and translated works. His titles include *The Laugharne Poems, Writing the Wind,* and *Drunk on Wine of the Beloved.* His literary archives have been recently purchased and are collected at Duke University, Durham, NC.

Malone T. Davidson, Penrose, NC, writes and paints in the mountains of North Carolina. She is originally from Atlanta, Georgia where she designed the look and logo, helped start, and edit one of the world's largest poetry and arts journals *The Atlanta Review.* Malone's poems and paintings appear in various spaces. She is the wife of a Baptist pastor.

Paul Donovan, Murphy, NC, is the author of *Ramblings of an Idiot,* a twenty year poetic autobiography. *Ramblings from Within* is soon to be published. Several of his essays have been published in various publications. He resides with his wife, Ann. He is an active member of the North Carolina Writers' Network West.

Mary E. Lynn Drew, Hayesville, NC, found N.C.W.N five years ago and began publishing poetry and prose. Her Heroic Woman series brought a NC Humanities Council Grant. Then play writing claimed her with a Josephine Niggle Playwright Award. She was a semifinalist at Mill Mountain Theatre. She has written twenty plays and produced eleven of them regionally.

Deborah Kinsland Foerst, Cherokee, NC, draws from the language, heritage, oral tradition and culture of the Eastern Band of Cherokee Indians, of the mountains, and of the South. She teaches eighth grade language arts at Cherokee Middle School. Her work has appeared in the *Asheville Poetry Review, Word and Witness, 100 Years of North Carolina Poetry, Cherokee One Feather,* and *Smokey Mountain Living.*

Joyce Foster, Cashiers, NC, says that these mountains are home to her even though she was originally from Oklahoma where her ancestors were relocated in the 1830's. She is blessed with family and friends who tolerate her eccentricities and make her laugh. She has been blessed by the love of a good man and poetry nurtures her soul.

Nita Gilbert, Murphy, NC, first learned she was a writer in a class taught by Nancy Simpson at the local Tri-County Community College. "Kathleen's Wedding" is her first published story. She says it is with great pride and much surprise that it was chosen for this anthology.

Dawn Gilchrist-Young, Cullowhee, NC, says that her formal education is patchy, her eating habits opportunistic, her family forgiving and mostly sane and her friends kinder and more numerous than she deserves. Reading and visiting wild places with her husband and daughter and solo runs on rainy days are her chief pleasures. She has no religion save nature.

Mildred Greear, Helen, GA, a poet/essayist, lives again where she spent the early childhood of her children, writing of that life in featured news and trade paper columns. She publishes in various journals and her song book, *Lullaby for Mary,* was the Georgia Printing Industry Association's design award for 2001-2002.

Steven Harvey, who selected the essays for this anthology, is the author of *Bound for Shady Grove* (Georgia), a collection of personal essays about his experiences learning to sing and play the traditional music of the Appalachian Mountains where he lives. He is also the author of *Geometry of Lilies* (South Carolina), *Lost in Translation* (Georgia) and he edited *In a Dark Wood: Personal Essays by Men on Middle Age* (Georgia). His essays have been published in *Harper's, The Georgia Review, Doubletake, The Fourth Genre and Creative Nonfiction.* He teaches at Young Harris College, serves on the Georgia Humanities Council and reviews books for the *Atlanta Journal/Constitution.*

Jerry R. Houser, Hayesville, NC, has enjoyed many careers in his life. He is a former lawyer and retired military officer, a licensed Commercial Pilot, Coast Guard Captain and presently a Realtor. He is also author of two published novels and numerous short stories and has others in progress.

Linda Taylor Kane, Hiawassee, GA, relocated from Atlanta to the north Georgia mountains with her family several years ago after discovering the region through her writing. She often draws upon her professional background in mental health nursing for perspective in her poetry. She is a member of the North Carolina Writers' Network.

Mary Michelle Brodine Keller, Hiawassee, GA, says that words are like small blue eggs that she incubates in hopes of giving them life that can touch and be felt. Her writings have been published in *The Mountain Lynx, Freeing Jonah III* and *Freeing Jonah IV.*

Blanche L. Ledford, Hayesville, NC, is a retired church secretary. She belongs to the Eastern Star and is an associate member of the Fraternal Order of Police. Her work has appeared in *Carolina Country,* and *Clay County Progress.* She served on the Clay County Heritage Book Committee.

Brenda Kay Ledford, Hayesville, NC, is a member of North Carolina Writers' Network and North Carolina Poetry Society. She is listed with *A Directory of American Poets and Fiction Writers.* Her work has been published in *North Carolina Humanities, Our State, Pembroke Magazine, Appalachian Heritage* and in many other publications.

Susan Lefler, Brevard, NC, works as a writer and editor for *Smoky Mountain Living.* Her poetry has appeared in *Asheville Poetry Review, Lonzie's Fried Chicken, The Lyricist,* and *Icarus.* Her poem, "In Mendel's Garden," won honorable mention in the 2002 Appalachian Poetry Competition.

Al Manning, Waynesville, NC, is a native of western Oklahoma. He is a retired instructor in microcomputer systems. Al has resided in Waynesville for the past twenty-two years. He spends his time fishing, playing tennis and doing computer projects for several non–profit organizations.

Mary Lou McKillip, Marble, NC, lives with her husband, Truman. She is a CNA Activity Coordinator and writer. She has two stepchildren, Diann and John McKillip and four grandchildren John, Jackson, Sophia and Maria. Her hobbies are dancing, singing, and piano. She has a strong belief in God.

Dick Michener, Waynesville, NC, is a writer, a teacher, and an entrepreneur. His stories and essays have been published in anthologies and print and online venues in the USA, Canada, and Australia.

Ralph B. Montee, Sylva, NC, is recently retired from Western Carolina University. For many years he has worked internationally in programs involving sustainable agriculture, the environment, and community development. His overseas experiences are often reflected in his poems. Poetry conveys him to the heart of time, place and people.

Pat Montee, Sylva, NC, after many years of living in far away countries came with her husband and daughter to yet another new country–the mountains of western North Carolina. People and their histories are her most compelling interests. She is also a gardener. When not turning soil, she cultivates memories.

Janice Townley Moore, Hayesville, NC, is a professor of English and Chair of the Humanities Division at Young Harris College. Her poetry has been published in *The Georgia Review, Prairie Schooner, Southern Poetry Review and Atlanta Review,* among others. She co-edited *Like A summer Peach* and was poetry editor of *Georgia Journal* for twelve years.

Ruth Moose, who selected the fiction for this anthology, is the author of *The Wreath Ribbon Quilt* and *Making the Bed* (August House, Little Rock), collections of short stories that first appeared individually in the *Atlantic, Redbook* and other magazines. She is also the author of four books of poetry, the most recent *Smith Grove*. She was awarded the North Carolina Writers' Fellowship, a McDowell Fellowship, a Carl Sandberg Award, the Robert Ruark Prize for Short Story and has received five PEN awards. She serves on the creative writing faculty at UNC-Chapel Hill.

Connie Quinn, Copperhill, TN, is a graduate of the University of Tennessee. She studied Botany and American Literature. She works at Quinn's Greenhouse in McCaysville. Her interests include Percherons, folk culture, local and family tales. The story in this anthology is a combined remembrances of Connie's Aunt Francis Brooks, and her own.

Estelle Darrow Rice, Marble, NC, is a retired Licensed Professional Counselor. Her interests in storytelling began as a child. She is a published short story writer and poet and has published literary publications such as *Appalachian Heritage, Journal of Kentucky Studies* and *The Back Porch*.

Mary Ricketson, Murphy, NC, writes poems to satisfy a hunger, to taste life all the way down to the very last drop. She gains perspective from family, friends, her Appalachian home in the woods, and her life's work as a counselor. She says writing places her in kinship with her own life.

Nancy Simpson, Hayesville, NC, is author of *Across Water* and *Night Student* (State Street Press). Her poems have been published in *Georgia Review, Prairie Schooner* and other magazines. She holds an M.F.A. in Writing, teaches Creative Writing, serves as the program director for N.C.W.N. West and is Resident Writer for Campbell Folk School.

Linda M. Smith, Hayesville, NC, moved from Florida to the mountains in 1988. She soon attended Nancy Simpson's creative writing class with her mother and discovered that she loved writing poetry and short stories. She learned a lot from the NCWN critique groups. She is currently working on a mystery novel.

Robin Taft Smith, Waynesville, NC, is a native of Greensboro, NC. Robin came to the southern Appalachian Mountains in 1976 as a student at Western Carolina University. He has been a psychologist at Thoms Rehabilitation Hospital since 1984 and expects to complete his Ph.D. in 2003. He and his wife have three children.

Dorothea S. Spiegel, Hiawassee, GA, now 80 years old, has written all of her life. She has edited newsletters and had articles published in newspapers in New York State, Florida and Georgia. She studied creative writing at Tri County College and at John Campbell Folk School and has published her own books of poems.

Ramona Layne Stylos, Brevard, NC, grew up in eastern Kentucky and has written about this in her memoir *Bearwallow Road, A Kentucky Childhood.* Before her retirement in the North Carolina mountains, she lived in Massachusetts and several foreign countries, raised seven children and worked as a school psychologist.

Shirley Uphouse, Marble, NC, and her husband retired to the mountains in 1995. Shirley is an AKC dog show judge. Her essays have been published in *The Australian Shepherd Journal* and *Dogs in Review* and in literary papers such as *Independence Boulevard* and *Appalachian Heritage.* She is a member of the North Carolina Writers' Network West.

John Webb, Del Rio, Tennessee, lives on the North Carolina state line near Max Patch. He is a freelance writer and heads a small publishing company, Rich Mountain Bound. John and his wife, Lori, farm and run a mountaintop retreat.

Emily Elizabeth Wilson, Sylva, NC, graduated from Western Carolina University with degrees in both English and Art with concentration in professional writing, book arts and printmaking. She loves to write and says she is itching to wander around for a few years living out of her backpack with pen in hand, yet she is determined to settle down here in these mountains.

Autumn Woodward, Franklin, NC, grew up in Western, NC with a deep love of the mountains and the outdoors, which is reflected in her writing. She plays old time fiddle, backpacks, whitewater kayaks, travels, writes, and likes dirt, bugs, people and open sky.

Doug Woodward, Franklin, NC, Is a long-time resident of the southern Appalachians. He and his wife, Trish Severin, built their own home in a secluded mountain cove, where their children were born and raised to appreciate the worth of all people, and the value of peace and simplicity.

Pat Workman, Hayesville, NC, was born in Franklin, NC. She is now retired and has been writing poetry for six years. Her poems have appeared in *Main Street Rag, Independence Boulevard* and in four volumes of *Freeing Jonah.*

Michael L. Wright, Brasstown, NC, was born in Dumfries, Scotland. He attended Herron School of Art of Indiana University. He now lives in Brasstown with his wife where they have raised three boys. He works as a designer woodworker.

Ila Yount, Waynesville, NC, is a published author of two novels. She is a native of Haywood County. After 25 years, she retired as Director of First Methodist Pre-School-Daycare. She taught Creative Writing at Haywood Community College for ten years. Her work has been published in *Wayah Review, Sunburst,* and she has edited three literary magazines.

With heartfelt thanks to the many supporters of this anthology, *Lights in the Mountains*, written by writers living in and inspired by the Southern Appalachian Mountains.

This project is supported by an $800.00 grant from the Clay County Historical and Arts Council with funding from the Grassroots Arts Program of the North Carolina Arts Council, a state agency.

The Clay County Historical and Arts Council donated $258.66.

This project is also supported with a $500.00 donation from the Cherokee County Arts Council.

The Cherokee Boys' Club donated $250.00

Benefactors Over $50.00:

Alan D'Arcy	Murphy, NC
Barrett's Body Shop	Hiawassee, GA
Fish Pond Cabins	Murphy, NC
Kathleen Crisp	Andrews, NC
Laurel Wood Photography & Framing	Murphy, NC
Ye Ole' Curiosity Shoppe	Murphy, NC

Patrons $26.00-$50.00:

Anonymous	GA
Anonymous	NC
Books Unlimited	Franklin, NC
Cocoon Interior Design	Brevard, NC
Daily Grind	Murphy, NC
David Hilton Realty	Murphy, NC
Dorothy Simpson Weatherford	Hayesville, NC
Dr. Edie Spence	Murphy, NC
Ingles Supermarket	Hayesville, NC
Jerry and Betty Anderson	Hayesville, NC
Kathskeller Coffee Haus	Franklin, NC
Marian Hobbie	Maggie Valley, NC
R. Neal and Barbara Ensley	Waynesville NC
Ralph L. Crisp Realty Co., Inc	Andrews, NC

Ralph Montee	Waynesville, NC
Shoe Booties Café	Murphy, NC
Town and Country Drugs	Hayesville, NC
United Community Bank of Hayesville	Hayesville, NC

Friends up to and including $25.00:

A1A Architect	Murphy, NC
Anonymous	NC
Country Cottage	Hayesville, NC
Dolores Piercy	Hiawassee, GA
Edward Jones Investments	Murphy, NC
Eloise D. Anderson	Warne, NC
Fannie Watson	Hayesville, NC
First Citizens Bank of Hayesville	Hayesville, NC
Freeman Gas	Murphy, NC
H. A. Manning	Waynesville, NC
Hayesville Hardware & Builders Supply	Hayesville, NC
Helen Crisp	Canton, NC
Highland Books	Brevard, NC
Irma McClure	Hayesville, NC
James Price	Hayesville, NC
Jane Young	Lake Junaluska, NC
Kathleen Roelof's Roberts	Murphy, NC
Mable Kitchen	Hayesville, NC
Macon Bank	Murphy, NC
Michael W. Davis	Andrews, NC
Mildred Greear	Helen, GA
Mrs. Oliver Yount, Jr.	Waynesville, NC
The Tool Shed	Waynesville, NC
Tri-County Computer Connection	Hayesville, NC
United Community Bank of Waynesville	Waynesville, NC
Virginia Wills	Murphy, NC